If You Can't Go Naked—
Here Are Clothes
to Sew on Fast!

If You Can't Go Naked— Here Are Clothes to Sew on Fast!

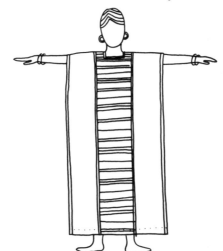

written and illustrated by Donna Lawson

GROSSET & DUNLAP
A National General Company
Publishers New York

ISBN: 0-448-01787-3

First Printing

Printed in the United States of America

The truth is that the very wearing of clothes has made the human body more sensitive to cold. We know, for instance, that the Patagonians, who lived near the southernmost tip of South America where the climate is severe, used to go about completely naked. When white missionaries came they insisted that the natives be decently dressed, and the race died out.

R. Broby-Johansen
Body & Clothes

Thanks to Mavis Dalton and Judy McGee, the ladies at the Metropolitan Museum of Art Costume Institute, and to Gordon Stone, the librarian, for showing me their folk designs.

Thanks to Caroline for the space in which to work, and to Jason for the title and to all my friends who lovingly sent me patterns and letters. And, hello Sara?

Contents

Introduction

I was sitting up at the Phoenix in Sugarbush Village the other day when Tim Lynch, this friend of mine, asked me what kind of book I was writing.

"I'm writing a sewing book, that tells how to get good-looking clothes on your back quickly, easily, and with little expense," I answered.

Tim looked at my favorite poncho (made out of an old navy blue camp blanket) and said, as though I hadn't answered him already, "I know. Your book tells how to lie down on an Indian print bedspread and cut a dress around you." Well he was right, you know.

I'm writing a sewing book that tells how to get good-looking clothes on your back quickly, easily at little expense. And in a manner of speaking I'm also *showing* the reader how to lie down on an old bedspread and cut a dress around her.

"Showing" is a key word here.

This book shows the reader how the designs *work* by using many illustrations instead of explanations, which by their nature are confusing. For this reason I'd suggest *looking* at the drawings of the garments before reading the instructions to get an "instant-flash" vision of how the garment is made. Then read the instructions. Fabric selvages are utilized whenever possible as finished edges. Iron-on tape is used and sometimes even fabric glue. Bound buttonholes, in fact, any buttonholes (except for a simple looped one on pp. 44-45) are eliminated, as are snaps, hooks and eyes, and zippers. In their place sashes, ribbons, and all kinds of ties are used for closures.

Using a tape measure and a little logic, most of the dresses and skirts can be made either longer or shorter. The tops can be made into dresses and most of the patterns can be made into children's clothes. Also many of these clothes can be worn by both men and women.

This book is roundly called a "sewing book," although the first sixteen patterns aren't sewn at all, but like garments in Eastern, Middle Eastern, and African countries, they are wrapped, then tied or pinned to keep them on the body. When seams *are*

1

used, they are kept to a minimum. Sometimes a whole garment is made with one seam.

Usually a geometric principle is applied, utilizing any square, rectangle, circle, or triangle to fit the body. A hole is cut through which you stick your head. Rather than using darts, gussets, or vents—all fussy stuff to my mind—ties, drawstrings, or elastic are used to pull the garment into shape.

This sewing book is as different from other manuals as clothes today are unlike those of a decade ago when I was a dress design student at UCLA and spent tedious hours sewing tiny anachronistic shaping stitches into horsehair muslin suit interfacings.

I hope you find this to be a friendly book. The patterns have been donated by friends. Their patterns demonstrate that anything goes as long as it works.

The novice won't learn meticulous sewing, as all the old rules have been thrown out. The long-time sewer won't learn anything new except how to throw out old concepts. But, both novice and long-timer will learn how to cut corners.

This is an intimate book as well as a functional one, looking upon sewing as a relaxing, pleasant, and creative experience. No one will use it without feeling great pride in creation.

1. Rock-Bottom Basic Tools

1. *By Machine or Hand?* Most of the patterns in this book are so easy to do they can be sewn by hand. (Basic hand stitches are illustrated on pp. 5-8.) So, whether you use a sewing machine or not depends a great deal upon your life style. Hand sewing can be very relaxing if you have the time. Machine sewing certainly goes much faster, but I know people whose sewing machines make them nervous. They just don't "take" to machines in any form. New sewing machines can be bought for less than $100. Secondhand or rebuilt machines cost even less. But be sure to buy from a reputable dealer. A sewing machine has an average life of twenty-four years. Mine has lived fifteen years and is a spry old thing. I'm sure it will live on until fifty.

2. *Table, Floor* or other cutting surface.

3. *Iron and Ironing Surface:* Particularly for this book, an iron is used to iron folds flat to save pinning them. And sometimes the iron is used to press back raw edges on the wrapped clothes. It is also used to press open seams on the wrong side so they look flat on the right side.

4. *Yardstick:* Necessary to draw long straight lines when the garment calls for it. Also good to get a straight hem. Ask a friend to stand it straight on the floor and evenly mark hem length you want by moving yardstick slowly around skirt with one end remaining on floor.

5. *6" Ruler:* Less unwieldy than the yardstick. Use it when short straight lines are required or short distances need to be measured.

6. *Tape Measure:* Two feet longer than a yardstick, its flexibility is needed for measuring around body; for example, to get hip measurement.

7. *Medium Size Scissors*

8. *Chalk or Pencil:* For marking your own paper or muslin pattern or for drawing out diagrams directly on fabric.

9. *Newspaper, Brown Wrapping Paper:* For those chary of cutting directly into fabric,

3

patterns in this book can be roughed out on paper. When paper (as with newspaper) is too small to "test" an entire pattern, tape several pieces together. Therefore you will need:

10. *Cellophane Tape:* Or masking tape

11. *Muslin:* To use if you wish to make sample garment to test fit.

12. *Assorted Needles:* Machine and/or hand

13. *Pins:* In a pin box or use:

14. *Pin Cushion:* Make your own: Cut two pieces of corduroy into 5" squares, seam up sides except for a small space through which you'll drop barley to fill. Sew up open seam.

15. *Needle Threader:* For those with astigmatism.

16. *Assorted Threads:* Cotton of different weights works for all the garments in this book. Size 50 or 60 thread is a good standard weight. For sewing on buttons (used once on pp. 44-45), buy slightly heavier weight thread. Buy colors as you need them. For most sewing jobs, use thread a shade darker than fabric as it usually sews up lighter than it appears on spool.

17. *Thimble:* Indispensable to some people. I've always found one clumsy to use, so over the years have toughened up my thumb, index, and middle finger like a guitarist toughens her fingers for the guitar frets.

18. *Seam Ripper:* Costs about 60 cents. Safer to use than a straight-edge razor.

19. *Plumb line:* This is a weight on the end of a string. It's dropped from top of seam to bottom to see that it hangs straight.

20. *Quick and·Easy Aids:*
   A. *Iron-On Seam Binding:* Good to turn a hem in minutes. Costs 35 cents for 3 yards. (Lie it flat on hem edge so half of it is on garment and the other half on hem and press with a hot iron (not too hot if fabric is synthetic.)
   B. *Iron-On Patches:* Mends torn areas of fabric.
   C. *Mending Tape:* Also for mending fabrics.
   D. *Fabric Glue:* Mends, but also can be used to quickly turn hems. Follow manufacturer's instructions. Be careful to use small amounts on thin fabrics, or it will soak through them. Also remember, it's hard to get the glue out if you want to change a hemline. Use nail polish remover to remove any glue that may have dribbled over onto areas of fabric where it is not desired. After glue has been used to secure fabric, a hem, for example, the garment can be cleaned or washed. The glue will remain intact.

21. *Optional:* Pinking Shears: Fine for finishing raw edges.

2. Hand Stitches

Note: Use a single thread about 18'' long for hand sewing, (except for gathering stitch, which takes double thread). When thread is longer than 18'', it tends to tangle easily. Knot thread on one end before you begin sewing. When you get to the last stitch sew over it two or three times to secure it. Then break or cut end thread to length of about 1/2 inch.

1. *Back Stitch:* Bring needle up through fabric. Instead of going forward (to the left), take a stitch backward (to the right) down through fabric to the right end of the first stitch. Bring needle up through fabric again about 1/4'' to left of starting point (depending on how long you want your stitch). Bring needle back down through fabric 1/4'' to the right. Repeat. Essentially, a back stitch is just as sturdy as machine stitching.

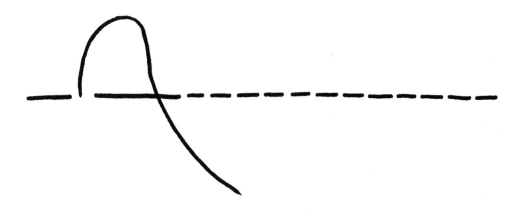

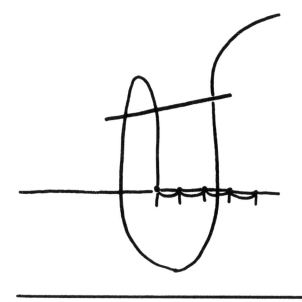

2. *Blanket Stitch:* Used to decorate edges, as armhole on Hopi Indian Dress, p. 59. Bring needle up through fabric 1/8" to 1/4" from edge. Carry thread over edge, down and up again through starting point. Before pulling thread tight, bring needle under the loop, so it forms a chain of knots along the edge. Each straight stitch is 1/4" to 1/2" apart.

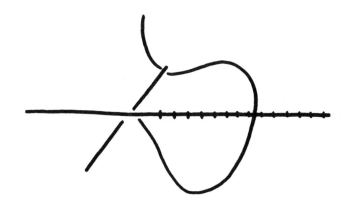

3. *Blind Stitch:* This stitch is used primarily to sew down the outer edge of an appliqué or facing and is almost invisible from outside. Bring needle and thread up from bottom of fabric just outside edge of appliqué or facing piece. Put needle into appliqué or facing piece 1/8" to 1/4" from edge and bring it up again just outside appliqué or facing edge. Repeat process.

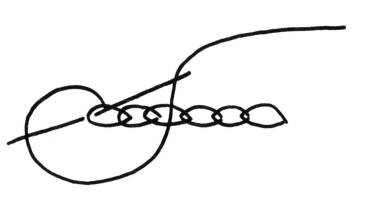

4. *Chain Stitch:* This is used to make flowers and other decorative stitches. Pull needle up to right side of fabric. Then, push it back through same hole this time bringing it up 1/8" away. Loop thread around end of needle before pulling it all the way through material. When needle is pulled through it will make a chain. Make next chain the same way by putting needle back into the last hole through which it came.

6

5. *Hem Stitch:* A friend is indispensable in the hemming process. Get him or her to put up the hem so it's even all around. Use a yardstick to get an accurate measurement. Cut off excess, if there is any, so hem measures standard 2 1/2" from bottom fold. Make sure hem is kept flat. Take a tiny stitch (catch only a couple of threads) in garment and bring needle diagonally through hem. Continue all the way around.

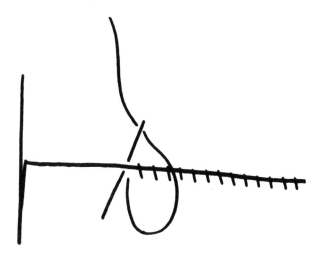

6. *Overhand Stitch:* Use this when sewing two pieces of leather or felt together. Join two finished edges (selvages, leather, vinyl, felt) with small close straight stitches made by bringing needle straight through two layers of fabric. Bring needle over fabric edges from back to front. Then insert needle in front, 1/4" from first stitch, through to back. Then, bring needle and thread over fabric edges from back to front again. This stitch is also used as trimming on edges, either two sewn together or a single edge.

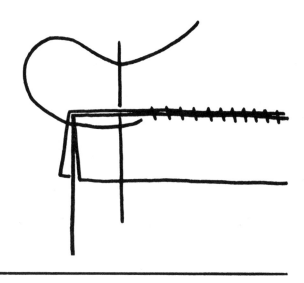

7. *Running Stitch:* This stitch is made by weaving small stitches evenly in and out of fabric. This or the back stitch can be used in lieu of a sewing machine. But, back stitching is much sturdier. Use small stitches for permanent seams, larger ones for basting. Basting is a stitch that holds two pieces of material together on an unpermanent basis; for example, to try garment on for fit. The running stitch is also used for gathering material together.

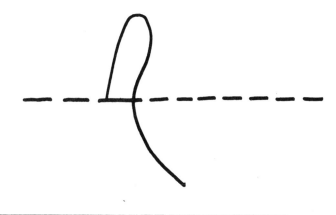

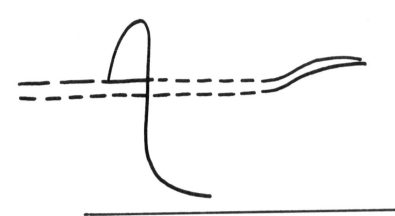

8. *Running Double Stitch:* This stitch is used to gather up fabric. (Use a double thread for extra strength, so it doesn't break when you are gathering up fabric.) Take several stitches (1/4" apart) up on the needle at once. Pull needle through fabric pushing fabric back against knot every few stitches. When gathering a long piece of fabric, make a double row of stitches about 2 1/4" apart, so if one row breaks, you still have the other with which to work.

9. *Tacking Stitch:* Tacking secures elastics or ties. Stitch an X five or six times in one spot through both elastic or tie and fabric.

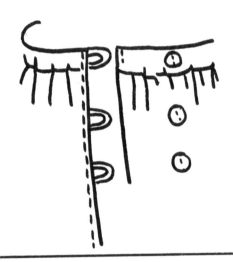

10. *Top Stitch:* Topstitching is usually sewn over a faced edge, on neckline, armhole, opening edge of dress, jacket, or skirt (see skirt front on p. 44), or on a French seam (see Grecian Tube, p. 51). Blue jeans are also finished with topstitched seams. The topstitching can be done with a small running or back stitch or with the longest stitch possible on your sewing machine. Topstitching can be put any distance from edge, but 1/4" is standard. Contrasting thread is very effective to use. Or make three or four rows of topstitching.

3. Cloth, Cloth Details and Cloth Type

Phaedre's Muslins: Phaedre, a friend living in Woodstock, New York, makes all her clothes from muslin, an inexpensive white-to-cream colored material that improves with each washing. If you shop around enough, you may find it for as little as 50 cents a yard. I've bought it that cheaply at the dime store. Mexicans make a good part of their clothes from muslin. It's a Mexican folk saying that to whiten these materials, "it is necessary for them to be rained on."

Dying Fabric: No silk is finer than Phaedre's muslins when she is finished with them. She transforms their plain colors into incredible hues, using ordinary packaged dye like Rit, taking the color as it comes from the box or mixing it with another shade. One outstanding periwinkle blue came about that way. Phaedre also tie-dyes, batiks, and block prints her muslins, processes easy enough to learn from borrowed library books. Then, like Mexican women, Phaedre richly embroiders and trims her muslins with decorative borders, ribbons, braids, and tassels. This same treatment can be given to other new or recycled materials.

Recycled Cloth: Materials need not be expensive. To my mind they should not be. One of my favorite garments, a caftan rather like Tralee's (p. 62), was made from an old burnt orange bedspread that had elephants marching around it. Tiring of the elephants on the bed, I transferred them to my body.

The Salvation Army is a wonderful place to go for recycled fabric. For the most part, they are free, or are sold at a nominal fee. My friend Lynn once found some drapes there with gigantic cabbage roses printed all over them. She cut them up into vests, lined them with velvet, and sold them at a handsome markup. Thrift shops, flea markets, garage sales, free stores, even trash cans are good places to look for cloth. I found an old lambskin coat in a bin at the corner of Lexington Avenue and Thirty-seventh Street in New York City, which I turned into a perfectly fine vest.

9

Other items, new or used, that can be turned into clothing include blankets, tablecloths, sheets, towels, curtains, afghans, quilts, dish towels. And old clothes can be used to make new garments. A tumble in a washing machine and a press with the iron usually pulls these materials into shape to cut up into garments, unless they are velvet, wool or the like and call for dry cleaning or hand washing. Stained areas can be cut away. Rips can be mended with iron-on tape. Large clothes can be cut down into small ones. Coats can become vests or skirts. (I once made a camel-hair skirt from a man's coat found in the Salvation Army.) Vests or skirts can be cut down into children's wear.

Patches: Recycled materials can be cut up into patches, as can leftover new materials. As my North Dakotan friend Ella Geist says, "Little patches into big things grow." (See Puff-Piece Vest, p. 142.) Several colorful patches can be sewn together (seams pressed out flat) to make a large piece of yardage. The floor-length cape on p. 106 would look fabulous in patchwork, provided it was lined to cover up the many rough seam edges inside. Patches need not be the same size or shape. They can be triangular, rectangular, square, even circular (like the Puff-Piece Vest). Patches on the same garment need not be restricted to one fabric, but can be velvet, wool, cotton, silk. Washables, however, should be sewn together, as should fabrics that must be dry cleaned. Hankies and bandannas sewn together grow into one large cloth. Pretty linen hankies make pretty linen blouses and dresses. A bunch of American Western bandannas, selling for about 25 cents each, piece together to make a skirt (see John Wayne skirt, p. 67).

New, Too: Although I'm an inveterate rummager, I do buy new cloth, too. And sometimes I splurge on something totally extravagant, but only sometimes. Dime stores and discount stores, when you sift through the gaudy and cheap often reveal beautiful little gems of cloth. I once bought three yards of 36" wide black, orange, yellow, and magenta printed Indian cloth for one dollar, the lot. In turn it became a wall covering, a dress not unlike the Fly-by-Night Dress (p. 164), and finally pillows for a tiny cottage I rented in Woodstock one summer.

Remnants: Terrific fabrics can turn up in remnant bins. Remnants are the material that comes off the bolt last, usually in funny sizes like 1 3/8 yards—all you may need. Sometimes I've bought the last 2 yards on a bolt and had another 1/2 yard thrown in free, so the salesperson didn't have to mark it for the remnant bin.

Lining Material: Lining fabric is generally inexpensive and makes nice clingy outer cloth. Rarely does anyone bother lining garments these days. My friend Sara bought some gray crepey lining with a distinct 1930's flavor to it at 3 yards for a dollar. Part of the fabric's character (and the reason for the low price) was the bronzy streaks at regular intervals where the sun had faded the edges of the fabric bolt.

Mill Ends: Throughout high school and college, I clothed myself with dresses and skirts made of mill ends, bought at outlet stores near the Los Angeles garment district. A yard of 54"-60" of men's very expensive woolen suiting (enough for a skirt) costs about a dollar. Because it was the last of a manufacturer's bolt, and not enough to clothe a moustached midget, it was "on sale."

Cloth Details

Grain: There are two grain lines in a piece of fabric, consisting of cross threads and lengthwise threads, each at right angles to the other. The cross grain runs from selvage to selvage, and the lengthwise grain runs the whole length of the fabric. Sometimes fabric has been stretched on the bolt so pulling a thread across from selvage to selvage will clearly indicate the true cross grain. So that a garment will hang straight on the body, it must be cut "on the straight" of the fabric, that is, both sides of bosom or hip part of garment must lay on the same cross thread. (In commercial patterns there is a line drawn to indicate the straight of the fabric.) Anyway, cloth should hang perfectly vertical on the body or your garment will veer to one side. There is an exception to this rule. Sometimes inexpensive materials have patterns stamped on them rather than woven into them. Under these circumstances you'll have to go with the direction of the fabric print rather than he grain. Sometimes this works fine as with the wrapped and tied garments. The voile I bought for my wrapped garments had a pattern printed on it "off grain." At other times fabrics are deliberately cut against the grain on the bias to give a garment a drapey 1930's look.

True Bias: The true bias is the diagonal between cross and lengthwise grains.

Selvages: These are the finished edges of fabric that keep it from raveling. Selvages are very important in this book, as they are often used in the diagrams to indicate placement of garments and clarify instructions. Perhaps more important, they are used "as is" to finish garments at hemline, armhole, neckline, backline, and so forth, places that conventionally call for facings or hems. But this is not a conventional sewing book.

Preshrinking: Most fabrics should be preshrunk, unless specifically labeled otherwise. When in doubt, it's best to hand rather than machine wash materials. The easiest way to preshrink cloth is to dip it in warm soapy water and hang it straight over a clothesline or the shower curtain rod. Generally, most linens and cottons may be washed. Silks and wools, and especially crepes should be dry

cleaned. Wool blends (20 percent nylon) should be preshrunk, but the most common blend, 65 percent dacron, 35 percent cotton will not shrink, is washable, and requires no ironing. Cotton knits and terry cloth, known to shrink more than 5 percent in washing, should always be preshrunk. Corduroys also have a slight potential for shrinkage.

Sizing: Many fabrics, muslin in particular, have sizing (a stiffening agent) in them. After washing the fabric, it becomes softer and more pliable.

Nap: Like a kitten's fur some fabrics (velvets, velours, corduroys, and terry cloths) have a soft hairlike surface that smoothly goes in one direction. The fabric "roughs up" just like a kitten's fur when your hand runs along it in the wrong direction. Fabric pieces should all be cut in the same direction, otherwise there will be a slight color change.

Cloth Type

Most of the materials used in this book happen to be soft, probably because of my prejudice for soft clingy fabrics. For economic reasons I also like fabrics that can be washed rather than dry cleaned. It burns me up to pay cleaning bills. Most of the woolen garments in this book can be safely washed in Woolite and cold water, then pressed with an iron, using a wet piece of muslin as a pressing cloth. It's hard to categorize these materials, as it's hard to categorize anything. Generally I'd say the materials fall roughly into:

Light Bodied

silky (real or synthetic) jerseys	muslin
	voile
cotton	lining silk or
cotton blend	rayon
batiste	

Medium Bodied

Thai silk cotton knit
synthetic crepe terry cloth
wool crepe velour
wool challis velvet
satin crushed velvet
wool knit wool jersey

Full Bodied

denim leather
corduroy suede
blanket weight felt
  wool

4. Notions or All the Little Extras

Appliqué Pieces: Cut and save patterns out of old cloth to appliqué onto new materials. I've saved an old chintz peony patterned slipcover for years, knowing I'll appliqué the flowers to some kimono or other someday.

Beads: Pretty little things to sew on garments.

Bias Tape: Use for decorative detail.

Bias Seam Tape: Use to reinforce seams at stress points. Also can be sewn to raw edge of hem before turning it up.

Braids: From soutache to elaborate decorative braids, striped, flowered, checked, metallic, scalloped, old and new. Carefully remove old braid from recycled clothing. Braids are used both decoratively and functionally. They edge sleeves and necklines so you don't have to hem them. Then too, you can catch your hem up and machine sew it through a braid placed 2 1/2" up from edge.

Buttons: Cut buttons off old clothes and reuse. Sew up a line of buttons of different colors for a decorative accent. Use big chunky beads for buttons. Buy baby buttons: mother-of-pearl rabbits, elephants, and bears. Look for antique buttons. My favorite are gargoyle heads made of molded cheese.

Crocheted Detail: If you crochet, or have a friend who does, collect and/or make up colorful pieces to use as decorative detail on garments. Old-fashioned crocheted lace doilies, dress collars, fichus, and so on, look superior on clothes.

Drawstrings: Buy or save anything that looks like it would make a pretty drawstring: twill tape, velvet cording, unfinished cording, covered cording, leather strips, peasant woven sashes, ribbon, bright yarns, drapery cords, or whatever.

Elastics: Great variety: from elastic thread, which can be used on a sewing machine, to 1/4" to 1", to widths of 4" to 5". There's an elastic for lingerie, for pajamas, another for waistbands and still others for additional things, in colors of white, nude, and black. There's a special polystretch chlorine-treated

13

nylon elastic that is used for bathing suits, like Little Bikini Bottom, p. 135.

Embroidery Threads: Come in varied colors, plus iridescent and metallic.

Eyelet Embroidery: Flat, ruffled, or with a place through which to run ribbon.

Fringe: Ball fringe, long Spanish shawllike fringe, wool fringe, all the fringe you like.

Lace: Old lace, new lace, stretch lace, insertion lace (to sew between two pieces of cloth), seam lace (to hem hems, if you want to be that fancy). The finest I ever found was a handmade lace curtain that was cut into pieces, and lovingly appliquéd all over a long velvet Christmas dress.

Piping: This is a bias tape over a fine cord, which is sewn into seams to make a pretty edging.

Ribbons: All kinds: grosgrain (to make Tote Bag, p. 141), velvet, satin, moiré, embroidered, and antique.

Rickrack: Zigzag woven trim with a "down-home" flavor.

Studs: Metal decorations with prongs to hold them into fabric, used mostly on denim and leather.

S. Facts A to Z

This section contains all those terms used throughout the book that you may or may not understand. Here you'll learn how to do some things that may be breezed over in later explanations. This is an invaluable section, read it now and refer to it frequently.

Appliqué: One shaped piece of fabric (a tulip, a duck) sewn on to another piece of fabric of a contrasting color. Edges of cut-out design are folded under 1/4" (clipped if necessary). Appliqué pattern is sewn down with a machine stitch or a blind stitch (see Hand Stitches, pp. 5-8). Used for decorative purposes *and* practical ones, like covering over a stain or rip in recycled or "on sale" cloth.

Casings: The fabric that is turned and sewn down 2 1/2" at top of skirt or pants waistline through which is drawn a drawstring or elastic. Casings around sleeve and neckline measure 1".

Center Back: The exact halfway point of back starting with first knob of spine at neck, down through the tailbone.

Center Front: The exact halfway point of front starting at collarbone, going between breasts to belly button.

Circumference: The line bounding a circle or other round surface, as cape on p. 106, or hat on p. 138. The circle's diameter is the straight line passing through the center of the circle from one side to the other. The diameter is found by dividing the circumference by 3.14, although being a mathematical moron, I cheat and round it off to 3. For example, say you're making a hat and need to draw the circle for the center of it. Measure the circumference of your head. If your head measures 22" around divide 22 by 3. That gives you 7, which is your diameter. You can always clip away a little fabric if your rounded-off measurement has made the area too tight. The radius is half of the diameter. This you would need if you were folding fabric four ways like a napkin and cutting a circle from the pointed folded edge. To get a semicircular measurement take circumference (for example, your waistline). Find diameter. Whatever that measurement is, use it to measure down from top of fabric on folded side. See skirt, p. 108.

Clipped Curves: Clips, either straight slashes or small pie-shaped notches, made almost to seam line at curve of armhole, neckline, crotch, or in facing seam or appliqué edge to keep those areas from pulling at the seam.

Donna's French Seam: I have been making this seam for years only to find out recently it's not bonafide French. Nevertheless, this is the way I make a French seam. (Check out another sewing book for the other version.) This seam can be made inside or outside of the garment. The Greek Tube (p. 51) is "French seamed" on the outside. Whether outside or inside, make a French seam by first stitching a regular 1/2" seam. Then press both seam edges to one side. Turn these seam edges under and inward toward first stitching just enough so they can be caught with another row of stitching. Press or pin in place. Topstitch. (See Hand Stitches, p. 5.)

Drawing through Elastics and Drawstrings: Used frequently in this book to draw together the shape of a garment. Different kinds of elastics and drawstrings have been listed in Notions, p. 13. Pin a large safety pin to the end of elastic or drawstring and push it through casing. Adjust elastic or drawstring around neckline, waistline, or arm for comfortable fit, leaving ample loose ends to tie a knot or bow. Tack elastic in place.

Ease Allowance: This is added to your body measurement, giving you room to "move around" in your clothes. The amount of ease allowed depends upon the garment.

Edging: When term "to edge" is used it means sewing a ribbon or other decorative trim over a raw edge at neckline, or armhole edge, etc., in lieu of hemming or facing it.

Embroidery: This is a decorative pattern made by using special stitches like the blanket or

chain stitch shown on p. 6. There are an infinite number of embroidery stitches; if you don't have a granny to teach them to you take out a library book on the subject. Embroidery stitches are great to make a garment look special, or like appliqués, to cover up rips or stains.

Facings: Usually you can sew ribbon to raw edges or hem stitch them back. But, sometimes you may want to face a raw edge. Cut a piece of fabric the same shape as the opening and about 2" to 3" wide. Cut facing straight if it is to hem a skirt where there is not enough fabric allowance to turn one up. With right sides pinned together, stitch facing to garment. Clip edges up to seam line in curved areas. Then press facing flat away from garment. Now stitch very close to seam line along facing side. This stitch is called a "stay stitch." Once facing is pressed in place this stitch will keep it flat so it won't roll toward right side of garment.

Fold (on the): When this book instructs you to cut a pattern "on the fold" it means placing the pattern on the edge where fabric has been folded to save having to cut two pieces, which then have to be seamed together. The back of a garment is usually cut on the fold.

Hem Allowance: Standard is 2 1/2".

Piece It: This refers to seaming one or several pieces of cloth together to make a whole when there is not enough fabric to cut a section "all in one piece."

Pinning: Straight pins are used to hold two pieces of fabric in place so they don't slip when you are cutting them. Pins also hold fabric in place while stitching it. Sometimes you can go ahead and stitch without pinning, but if material is slippery it's tricky. Generally, it's best to put pins at right angles to fabric edge, so they don't interfere with the needle and thread. Sewing machine needles are particularly susceptible to breaking when they hit a misplaced pin.

Plaids, Stripes, Prints—Matching Them Up:
To save your sanity avoid unbalanced plaids and stripes, which are difficult to match up evenly when you want to cut out your pattern. Balanced plaids, stripes, and prints should be carefully matched on all sides when fabric is doubled. Sometimes pinning fabric at edges keeps patterns carefully placed together.

Raw Edge: As opposed to a selvage, which is woven, this edge is made by a scissor cut or by ripping along the grain of the fabric.

Reinforcing: When stress is put on a seam, particularly the curved area under armhole or crotch, you may want to strengthen or reinforce it by sewing a piece of seam binding over that area.

Right Side and Wrong Side: In that order, refers to the finished and unfinished sides of fabric.

Seam Allowance: Standard is 1/2". (Standard for commercial patterns is 5/8".)

Vents or Slits: These are open areas usually about 6" up side seams of dresses, skirts, and blouses to allow for extra ease of movement. Vents are sexy, too, as they usually bare a little skin.

MEASUREMENT CHART

A. Bust
B. Waist
C. Hips at 4" below waist
D. Hips at 7" below waist
E. Hips at 10" below waist
F. Shoulder to point of bust
G. Shoulder to waist back
H. Across upper back
(from shoulder to shoulder)
I. Across upper chest
J. Around upper arm
K. Around forearm
L. Around wrist
M. Shoulder to elbow
N. Shoulder (around elbow) to wrist
O. Around upper thigh
P. Around calf of leg
Q. Around ankle
R. Around hand

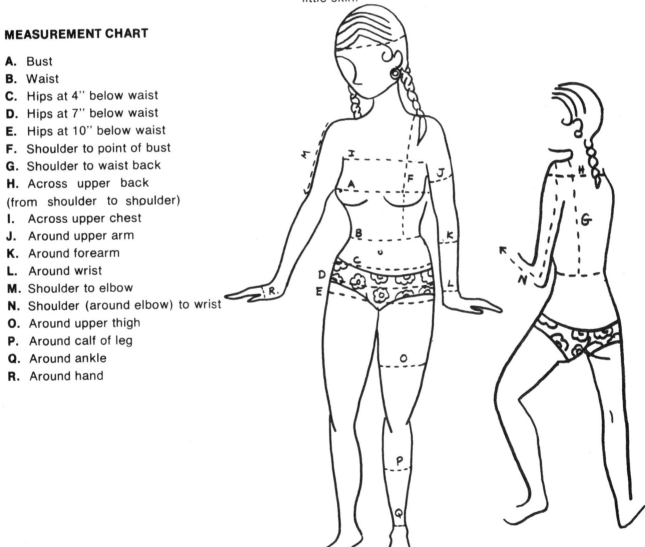

17

6. Clothed without a Stitch

The concept of making clothes without sewing them is not new. Many women in other cultures have done this for centuries. African women have always created beautiful clothes that simply wrapped, tied, or pinned on. So have the Burmese, Balinese, Indonesian, Eastern and Middle Eastern and Thai people.

To demonstrate this, the New York Metropolitan Museum recently presented a collection of unsewn clothes. Now unsewn clothes have caught on with Western people who traditionally have worn only tailored garments. Capitalizing on his trend, a New York designer has recently marketed a $35 slinky piece of cloth that can be wrapped, tied, or pinned on six different ways. I've personally tied on several of the garments in the following section with $1.50 worth of voile (3 yards at 50 cents a yard).

In many countries the material for wrapped garments was, and still is, woven an exact width and length, usually standardized to a particular size, just as we get clothes sized 8, 10, or 12. Sari cloth, for example, is generally woven to a length of 6 yards and about 45'' to 46'' in width. Woven ethnic fabrics are usually available in fabric shops or shops that specialize in a particular nation's imported goods, although over-the-counter fabrics work fine for most of the following unsewn clothes.

The point of wrapping, tying, or pinning on garments is not to attempt to imitate any particular ethnic group. Some of the styles have been liberally adapted for Western tastes. The point is that these techniques offer a way to create unique, good-looking garments in a very short time.

Selvages, the finished edges on both sides of a fabric width, save the wearer from having to hem either at waist or hemline. The raw edges on either end of the fabric (say it's 3 yards) fold or tuck under somewhere on the garment. Raw edges can be ironed under or pinked with pinking shears.

Soft pliable fabrics naturally are best to wrap, tie, or pin on the body. Soft cottons, broadcloth and knits, polyesters and silks that will hold a knot, and synthetic and wool jerseys are ideal.

Most of these wrapped and tied garments will stay on without pinning them. But, if the material is particularly silky and slippery and you feel insecure about its "holdability" secure the wrapped garment with costume jewelry. Or use an ordinary safety pin, if it can be concealed under the fabric.

Betty Grable Scarf Top

1. Two large scarves the same size are needed.

2. Fold scarves in half diagonally. The fold goes under the bosom.

1.

2.

3. Tie two scarf ends together so they knot between breasts.

4. Tie two scarf ends at back of neck. Tie remaining two at center back.

3.

4.

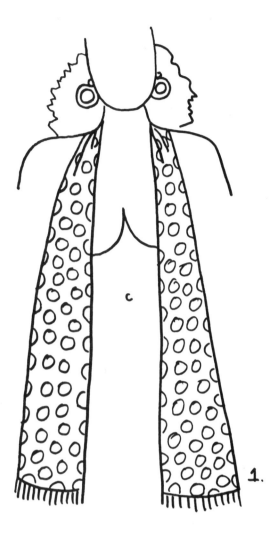

Crossover Scarf Wrap

1. Take a very long rectangular scarf, about 1 foot by 2 yards long. Find the center of scarf and place at back of neck.

2. Bring long ends around to the front and cross them just above bosom. Catch one breast in each end of the scarf. You may want to pin the front to keep scarf from riding up.

3. Tie scarf ends behind your back.

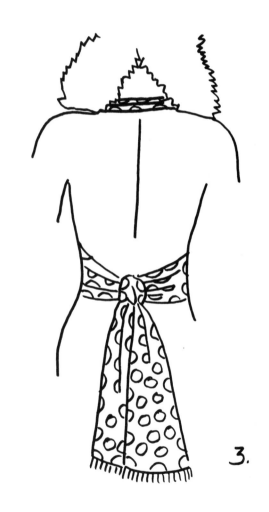

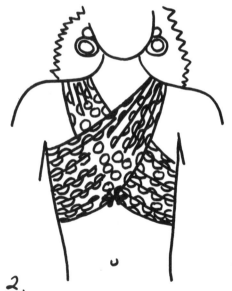

Two Scarf Tie-On

1. Use two scarves: a large square one folded diagonally and a long rectangular shape.

I.

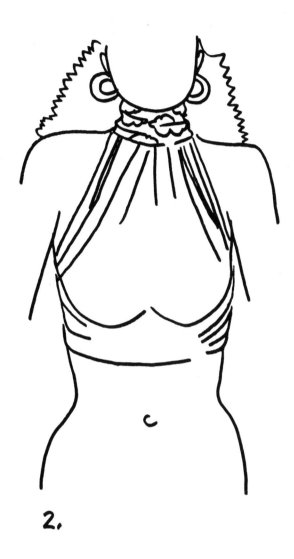

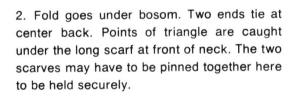

2. Fold goes under bosom. Two ends tie at center back. Points of triangle are caught under the long scarf at front of neck. The two scarves may have to be pinned together here to be held securely.

3. Long scarf knots at back of neck. Ends flow loose.

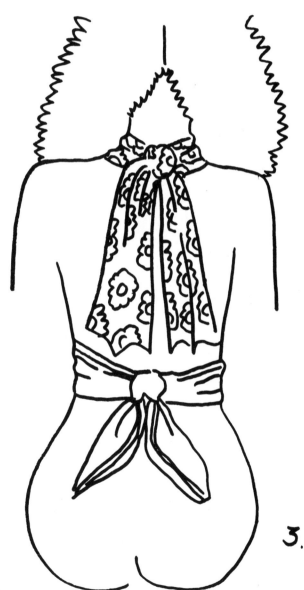

One-Knot African Halter

1. Use 2 yards of soft cotton, 45" wide, folded lengthwise.

2. Selvage edges point toward waist. Folded edge points toward neck. Center fabric at front covering bosom. Bring loose ends around back and down toward waist. Knot at center back. Tuck under loose ends of cloth.

Selvage

1.

2.

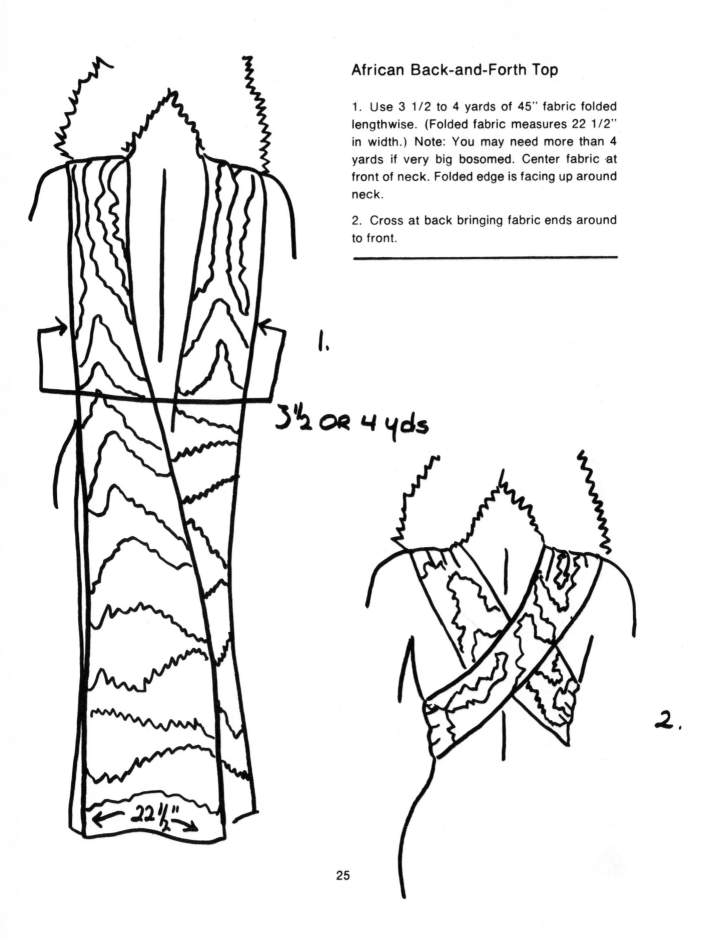

African Back-and-Forth Top

1. Use 3 1/2 to 4 yards of 45" fabric folded lengthwise. (Folded fabric measures 22 1/2" in width.) Note: You may need more than 4 yards if very big bosomed. Center fabric at front of neck. Folded edge is facing up around neck.

2. Cross at back bringing fabric ends around to front.

1.

3½ OR 4 yds

22½"

2.

3. Fan out fabric folds to cover bosom. Cross one side of fabric over the other. Pull ends to back.

4. Knot fabric at center back of waist and tuck in ends.

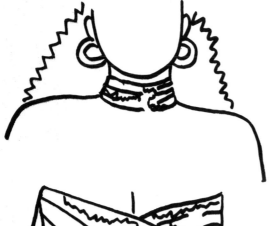

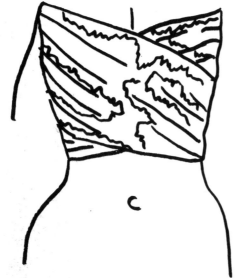

C

3.

4.

Nigerian Knotted Skirt

1. Use 3 yards of soft, pliable 45" wide fabric. Less yardage works if hips are small. Generally you should allow for double your hip measurement and add another yard. If hips measure 38 inches, even 3 yards barely make it twice around with room for the knots. Stand with legs spread apart, so there is enough "give" in the wrapping of the skirt so you can walk later. Hold one end of fabric at right side of waist. Wrap fabric around front of body, then wrap around to back, until you reach right side again. Pull up a tab of fabric (point A) and tie to end piece with which you started.

2. Wrap fabric around front, then back of body again. Tuck loose end into knotted right side. Fabric will sway out seductively on that side. The motion of the skirt looks great when you walk. Any one of the previously illustrated halters looks terrific with the Nigerian Knotted Skirt.

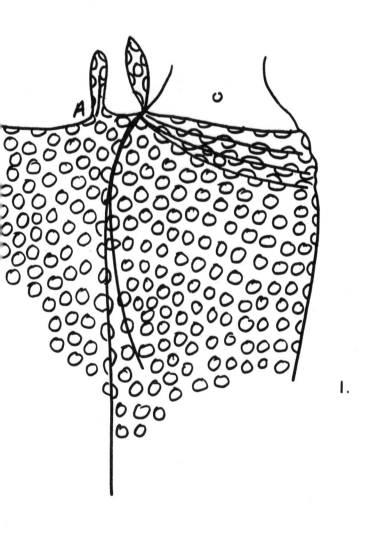

1.

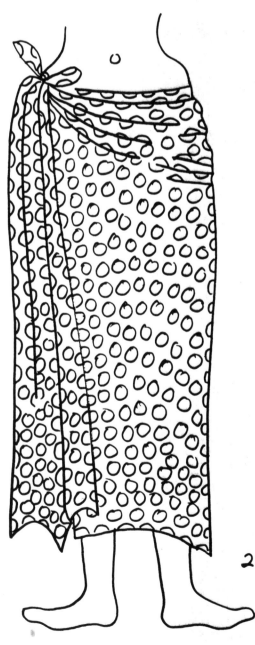

2.

Samoan Fantasy Dress

1. Take 3 yards of 45" fabric. Center it at middle of back. Pull the cloth toward the front pulling up two tabs to knot at bosom.

2. Knot fabric at center front over bosom. Folds cascade down front. Great to wear if you're pregnant. All that room up front.

1.

2.

Bustle Up Skirt

1. Center 3 yards of fabric at waist, center front. Fold fabric down at waistline to adjust length. Bring ends around to back and knot. All that fabric pulls tight around thighs and "bustles up" in back.

1.

Ghana Getup

The cloth for this costume, usually woven in Africa, is made so edges can be used for decorative borders. Most likely, it will not be easy to get fabric that is bordered all the way around unless you find the right twin-size bedspread. On the other hand, the border isn't necessary, any plain or printed fabric will do. Use a fairly stiff material if you want to give nice edges to the pleats, but a soft cloth works fine too.

1. Two yards will fit most women up to about size 12. At size 14 you may need 3 yards. Hold beginning edge of fabric at left side under arm. Bring fabric over bosom and around back until you return to point A. Secure fabric at this point with a safety pin, keeping safety pin hidden.

2. Bring remaining fabric to center front and pleat. Conceal raw edge in last pleat. Tuck pleats into dress at center front. They will usually hold at this point on their own. To be extra cautious you can use a costume jewelry pin.

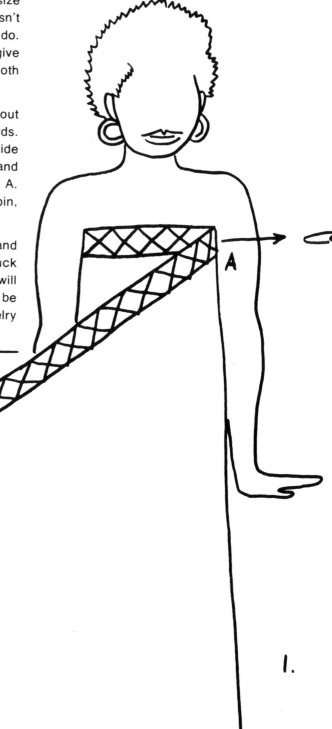

A

1.

2.

The Topsy Turban

1. Use 2 1/2 to 3 yards of 45" wide fabric. Fold lengthwise. Put selvage ends at base of neck; center fabric at back of head. Pull rest of fabric up toward forehead and cross ends there. Then bring fabric ends toward back. At back start twisting both ends together around right side of head.

2. The twisting creates a "rope of fabric" that extends from center back of head to fabric ends.

3. The "rope" end comes around from the right side and tucks into center front.

32

A Thai Panung

In Thailand, one standard length of fabric is 110" (108" is 3 yards) x 40". This fits men and women who both wear the panung for everyday wear. It is made of hand-loomed Thai silk, expensive in this country, but great cloth to use for your panung if you can find it.

1. Use 3 yards of 45" fabric. Center cloth at back so it completely covers your fanny. Pull fabric ends around to front and loop one end over the other, keeping both ends even.

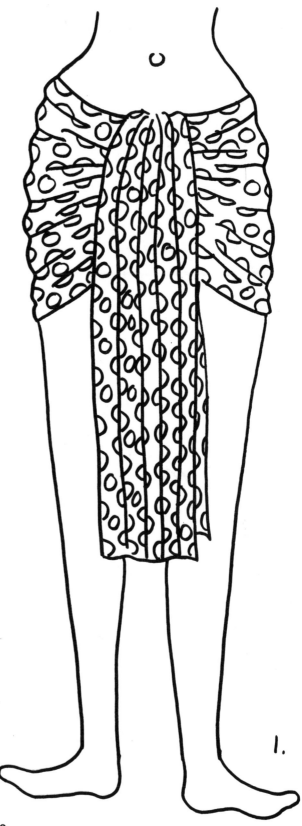

1.

33

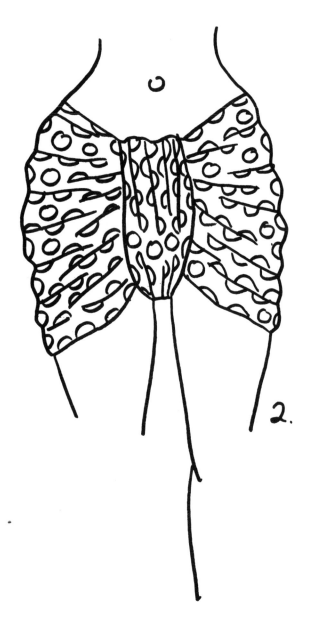

2.

2. Pull cloth between legs.

3. Tuck ends of cloth into top of panung in back. Adjust fabric so it is wrapped tightly enough to hold secure, yet draped loosely enough so it covers your crotch.

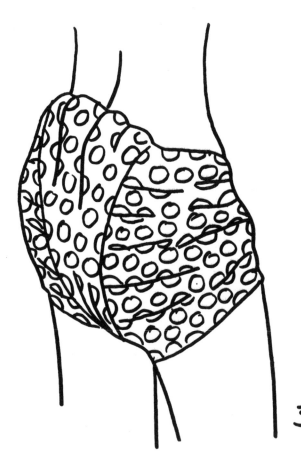

3

Tie-On Dress One

1. A soft, stretchy synthetic jersey works best for Dress One and Dress Two (below). Soft cottons or cotton blends can be used, too. Use 45" wide fabric. Selvage end at bottom serves as hem edge. Selvage at top makes a finished edge around neck line. Length of cloth varies from 60" to 70". This generally covers hip sizes from small (about 35") to large (about 45"), depending upon how much extra drape you want in back. Hold top of fabric (45" down, 60"-70" across) with both hands, grabbing a tab of cloth about 12" from either side of center front.

2. Tie ends behind neck. Drape front into a cowl neckline. Cross one side of excess fabric over the other side in back and fasten with a large decorative pin.

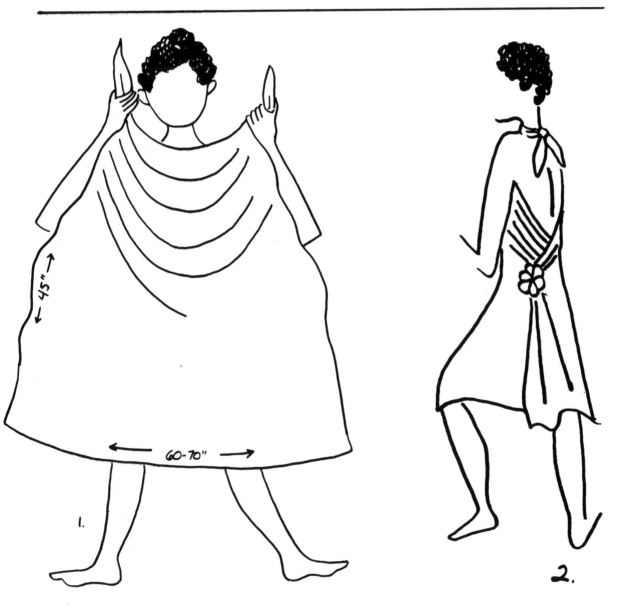

Tie-On Dress Two

1. Use same type fabric as used for Dress One: 45" wide, 60"-70" in length. Again selvages serve as hemline and edging around neck and backline. Center fabric at back. Bring it under arms.

2. Cross it over in front. Pull ends of fabric up. Tie ends together behind neck. Smooth drape of fabric in front so it hangs evenly. Every body is a little different so it may take a few adjustments in tying and draping fabric until it looks just right for you.

East-West Sari

Saris never go out of fashion and never need any alterations. They even become maternity wear. Remember when you wear a sari to take tiny steps—something to get used to if you usually stride. This sari is the modern twentieth-century variety worn for everyday occasions. It's called the Nivi Sari. Indian sari cloth is always woven with decorated ends, one more elaborate than the other. The end is traditionally called a "pallav." And Pallavi is a girl's name.

1. Use 45" wide fabric, 6 yards of it. Any soft cotton or silk will do. It need not be the traditional woven sari cloth. A long petticoat with a drawstring drawn through the waistline is usually worn under the sari. The petticoat is worn for reasons of modesty, but it is also functional. The petticoat's drawstring secures the sari waistline. A petticoat isn't entirely necessary, however, particularly if you aren't modest. A 1/2" wide grosgrain ribbon can be tied around the waist so the sari can be tucked into it. A little past center front tuck one end of sari cloth into ribbon. (How far you tuck the end into ribbon depends upon what length you want the sari to be.) Pull the rest of fabric around your back and toward front until point A reaches point B. Pull point A away from body with right forefinger. Spread thumb in toward your waist about 4" from your forefinger (point C). Start pleating by bringing fabric over forefinger and under thumb. Do this six times, moving finger and thumb for next pleat each time, all the while holding completed pleats with the rest of the fingers of your right hand. Have patience. The results are worth the effort here.

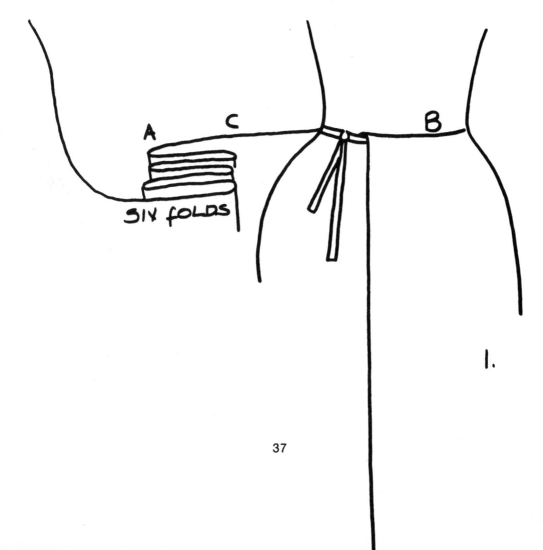

37

2. Holding pleats together as one, tuck them into grosgrain ribbon so they line up with point B.

3. Bring the rest of fabric around left side to back and under right arm.

4. Continue to bring fabric around to front and drape over left shoulder so it flows from there down your back. Wear the sari bare shouldered or with a tight short-sleeved little top. Indian women wear a special top called a "choli."

SIX FOLDS
TUCKED IN

2.

3.

38

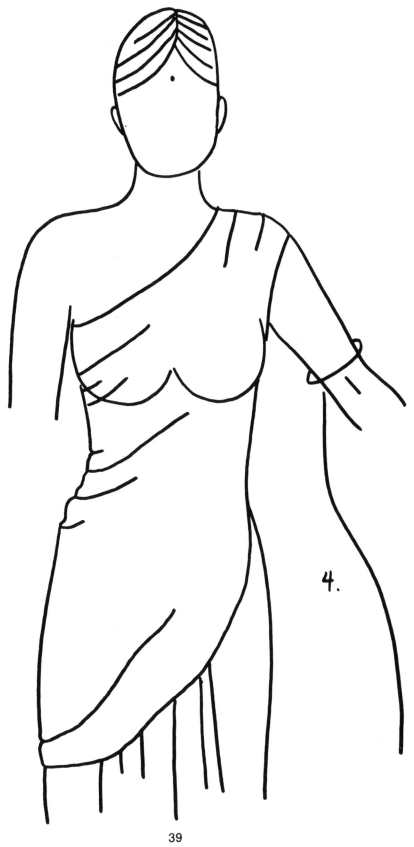

4.

7. A Seam in Time Saves Nine

When you have to sew more than nine seams, it sometimes gets to be a bore. One lazy summer afternoon, I sat with a group of fine ladies around Mary's old round oak table in her glass house up on Byrdcliffe Mountain in Woodstock, New York, and as enlightened and liberated as all claim to be, we exchanged views on a very old, traditionally feminine subject—sewing.

Belonging to that freewheeling group of people who roundly call themselves artists, we never have enough money or time. Never enough time because we spend most of it worrying about how we will make enough money to survive so we can have time. Anyway, we all loved fabrics and sewed to make pretty things and save money. Just as an exercise we spent a full two hours paring sewing down to its simplest elements—one seam, two seams, and some gossip.

This section is basically a compilation of that afternoon's talk and the garments sketched out and subsequently made. As this book progresses there will be some garments that will require more seams than others, but these clothes are kept to a minimum. An hour is about the maximum time spent sewing any garment. I've cut that time in half by liberally using selvages as finished edges for hems, arm holes, and so forth, as has already been demonstrated with the wrapped clothes. But I've even committed more of a cardinal sin (in my Granny's book) by using iron-on seam binding and—yes, I'll even admit to this—fabric glue (E-Z Magic Mender is one) to finish hems and other raw edges.

The first garment in this section has one seam.

One-Seam Jingle Bell Skirt

1. Use one piece of material that measures the width of your hips plus ten inches, or more than that if you are thin and can take the bulk. Make the skirt as long as you want measuring from waist down. Allow 5" extra: 2 1/2" to make casing for drawstring at top, and 2 1/2" for hemline.

2. Seam together two raw ends of cloth, leaving about a 12" slit at bottom. Hem bottom with hemstitch. Stitch casing on sewing machine or hemstitch it. At top seam reopen a slit on outside big enough to pull the drawstring through.

3. Thread through a braided cord, and *voilà* it's a skirt. For decoration attach small Indian bells, which jingle jangle at the ends of the drawstring.

1.

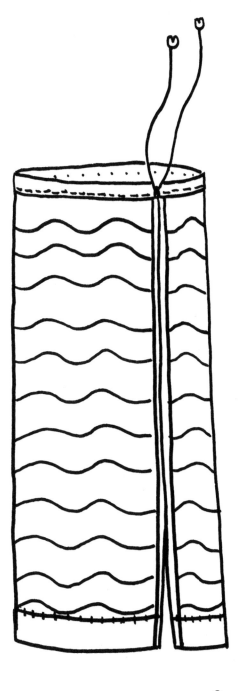

2.

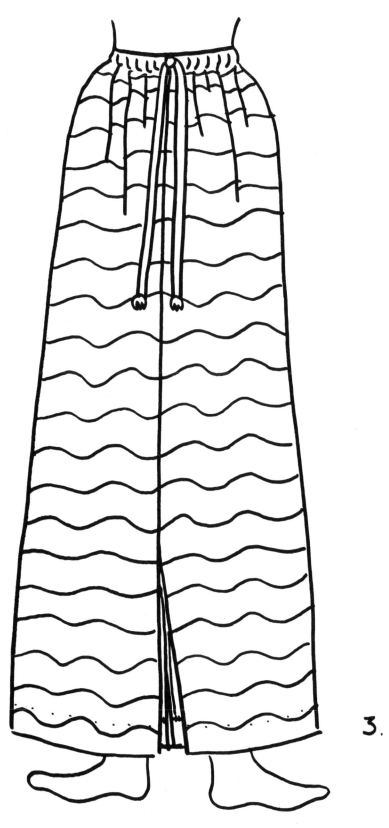

3.

One-Seam Button-up Skirt

1. Use 2 yards of 36" wide fabric for short skirt, 2 1/2 yards for a long one; 12 buttons for a short skirt, 25 for a long one. Skirt is made of wool jersey, but any fairly soft pliable cloth will do. Cut it to any length you want, allowing 2 1/2" for turn at top and another 2 1/2" for hemline.

2. Seam two selvages together. This will be center back. On left side at front, press under a 2 1/2" hem and hemstitch. On right side, measure a 3" wide strip down length of fabric and cut this piece. Lie the strip on piece from which it was cut with right sides together and raw edges together.

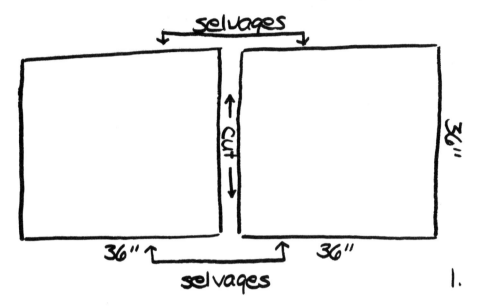

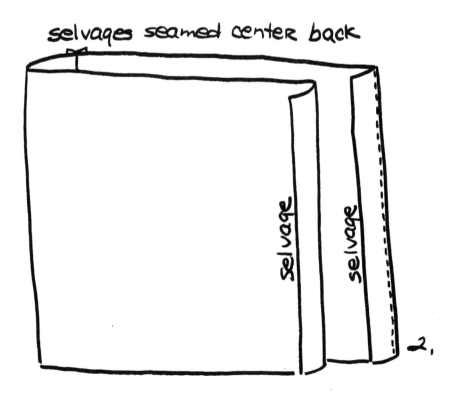

3. Starting at top, stitch 1/2" seam down 2 1/2". As you continue to seam, begin to sew buttonhole loops into inside of seam, spacing them about 1" apart. Use soutache braid (available at notion counters) or narrow elastic cut to a length that will snugly catch buttons when the loops are securely sewn into seam. Allow about 1/2" on either end of loop to extend into seam.

4. Press seam open.

5. Turn facing inside and press. Hemstitch facing to skirt on selvage edge.

6. Now, turn under 2 1/2" allowance at skirt top to make a casing, using hem stitch, and run elastic through it. (See Facts A to Z, p. 15.) Pull elastic, gathering skirt until it is 2 1/2" bigger than waist to allow for front lap where it will button. Tack elastic in place. Top stitch along right front the length of the skirt. First button loop should be at top of skirt. Two and one half inches from left edge of skirt begin to sew buttons so they align with buttonhole loops.

7. Turn up hem and hemstitch. When skirt is finished you may want to leave a few buttons undone at bottom. It's sexier that way!

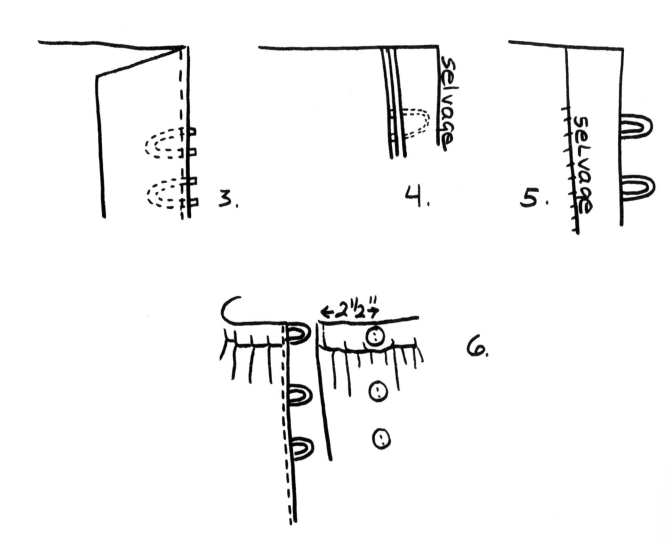

7.

Three-Way Convertible Skirt or Dress

The essential design features of this garment are its convertibility and the 6" opening that is left in the back or in the front. (It's in the back when the dress or skirt ties in the back and it exposes a bosom cleavage when the dress ties in front.) The opening can be longer or shorter, depending upon the lustiness of your nature.

1. Use 3 yards of 45" wide fabric. This will give you 90" of gathers around the waist or bosom, however you wear it. It's best to use soft thin material so garment won't be too bulky. For less bulk, use less fabric. 1 1/2 yards of 45" wide fabric can be used, merely seaming it once and allowing a gap.

Cut fabric to length you want from waist to hemline, allowing standard 2 1/2" hem. When ankle length skirt is pulled up and tied around bosom it will become a midi. Seam selvages together on either side. But, leave a 6" gap or longer on one selvage edge. Gather up top of skirt (by hand or machine) until it fits waist, except for a 2" gap. For example, if waist

measures 26", draw gathers in to 24" to make sexy gap. Naturally, the gap will be wider than 2" when skirt is drawn up over bosom and either exposes back or front cleavage.

2. Waist tie measures about 9" wide and about 6 yards long. One and one half yards of 36" wide contrasting material should be sufficient to make the sash if you "piece it" (sew parts of it together to make a whole). If you want sash to be in all one length you will have to cut it from 6 yards of fabric.

3. You'll need 3 yards of fabric to make sash from two pieces.

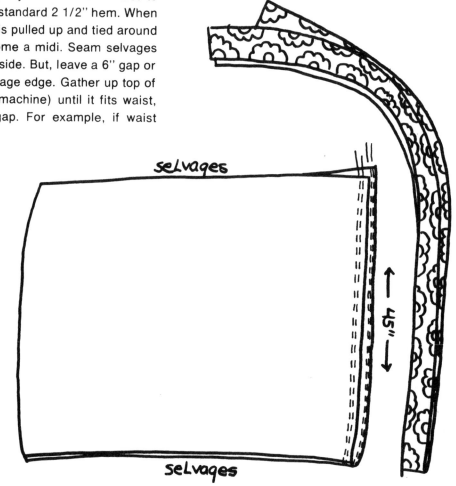

selvages

45"

selvages

1.

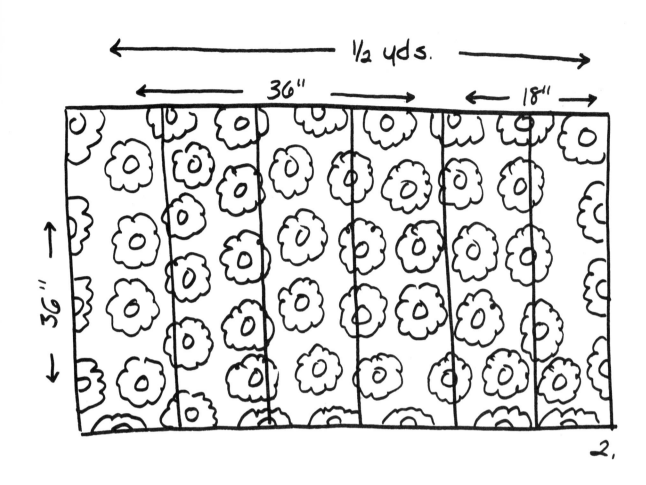

½ yds.

36"

18"

36"

2.

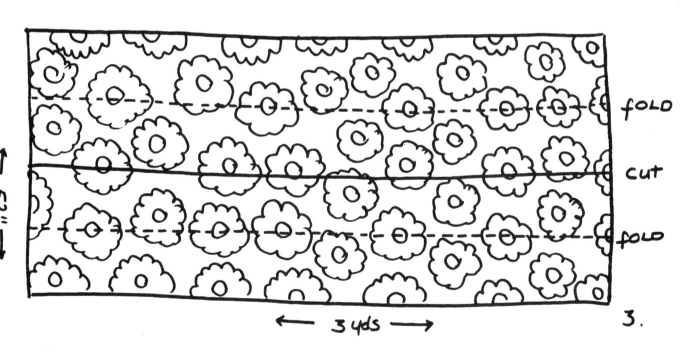

fold

cut

fold

62"

3 yds

3.

4. Hem skirt to standard 2 1/2". Sash ties into an enormous bow at back of waist. The gap (6" or longer) in back shows skin through it.

5. Or tie sash between shoulder blades. Figure 5 shows how dress would look with lower cleavage.

6. Dress ties in front with low cleavage.

5.

6.

Congolese Tube Skirt

This skirt is based on a traditional African style.

1. Use 2 yards of 36" wide fabric. Seam raw edges together so it forms a tube. Selvages are at top and bottom. Use selvages for finish at top and bottom or turn under standard 2 1/2" hem on top and bottom and hemstitch as shown in Figure 1 (inside of skirt).

2. Tie a 1/2" wide grosgrain ribbon around waist. Step into tube. Pull fabric forward and fold into two pleats that turn inward. At center front, tuck pleats into ribbon. The rest of tubular skirt should hold tight around back of waist. For extra security pleats can be safety pinned to ribbon waistband.

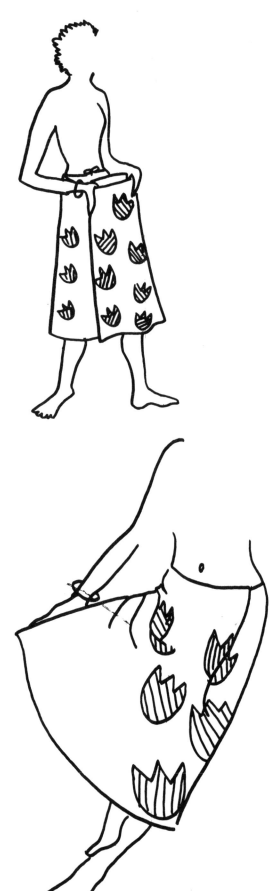

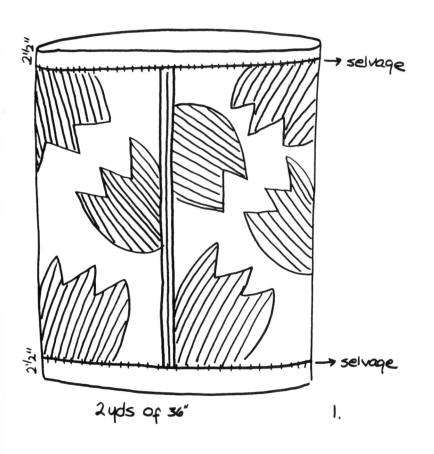

2½"

selvage

2½"

selvage

2 yds of 36"

I.

2.

50

Grecian Tube

This dress is a rendition of a chiton (the ancient Greek tunic worn by both men and women). It looks lovely in soft muslin or cotton velour, but any drapey material will do.

1. Use 2 yards of 45'' wide fabric (45'' around, 72'' long). Make a French seam (see Donna's French Seam, Facts A-Z, p. 16) with selvages on right side of fabric to make a tube. Turn 2 1/2'' down at top and hemstitch on finished side of fabric. Turn under a 2 1/2'' hem at bottom.

2. Pull tube up over body. Turn down top edge about 15'' and hold under arm. Hemstitching will now be hidden underneath it. You may embroider or decorate this turned over top edge if you like.

3. Pull up a part of this 15'' section and pin over each shoulder. Allow enough armhole room on each side for comfort. Use decorative pins to hold Greek tube on shoulders.

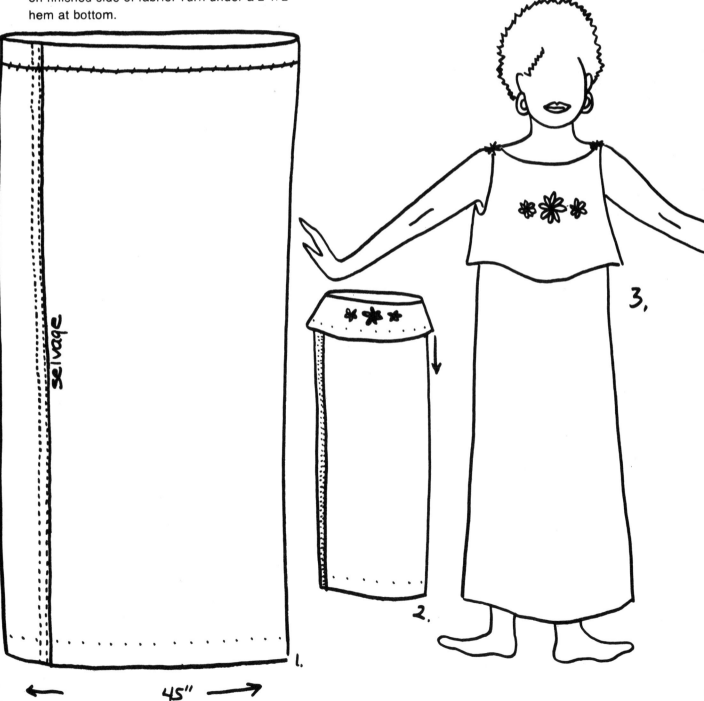

selvage

45''

Two-Way Elastic Skirt or Dress

1. The idea of this skirt is that it can be worn at the waist or pulled over the bosom to make a dress. The first version can be made from one bath towel, a standard sized one, measuring 24" x 47". The bath towel is seamed up the front. A 2 1/2" turn is sewn down around the top so elastic can be run through it and securely stitched down.

2. The midi length version of this can be made by seaming together raw edges of one yard of 45" fabric, so selvage edges are at top edge and hemline. As with bath towel version, elastic is run through the top to draw fabric together. The bottom selvage serves as the hem.

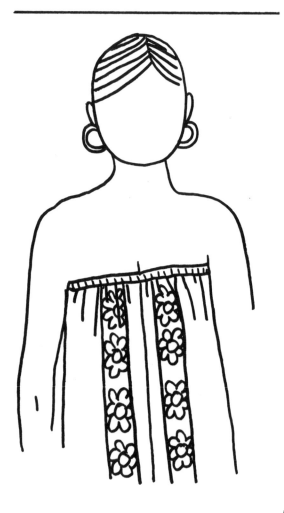

52

2.

Bath Towel Top

This towel concoction is most serviceable. Not only does it go with the bath towel skirt or blue jeans, but you can also dry yourself with it.

1. Take a towel 24" x 47". Fold it in half across width. Measure to center and cut 7" out on each side of that point so you have a 14" slit for neck. Turn back raw edge of neck slit and hemstitch.

2. On inside of folded towel, stitch up sides allowing enough space on each side (approximately 12") for arms to pass through comfortably. Leave open vents about 6" on each side of the bottom.

3. Turn towel right side out—presto a towel is a top!

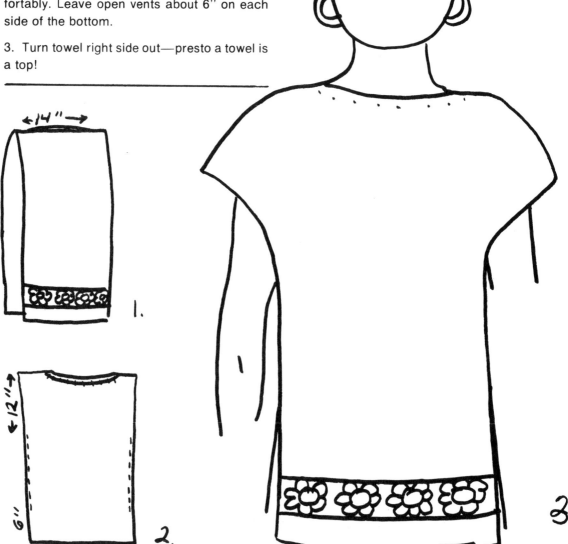

On-the-Fold Top

Here's another presto top that can be lengthened to make a dress.

1. Use a 54" square of fabric (woolens and wool blends usually come in this width). Fold fabric in half, widthwise, right side out. Find center of folded edge, now measure out 5" on either side to make a neck opening 10" wide. Cut 3" down toward hemline on either side of 10" allowance for neckline. Then cut away a rectangular section to make neckline opening.

Next, measure down 11" from fold then in toward center 15" on either side of fabric. Cut this 11" x 15" rectangle out on each side. These measurements allow for a 1/2" seam all the way around underarm and side. Slit underarm corner 3/8" as shown in Figure 1. Turn top inside out. Seam sleeves and sides.

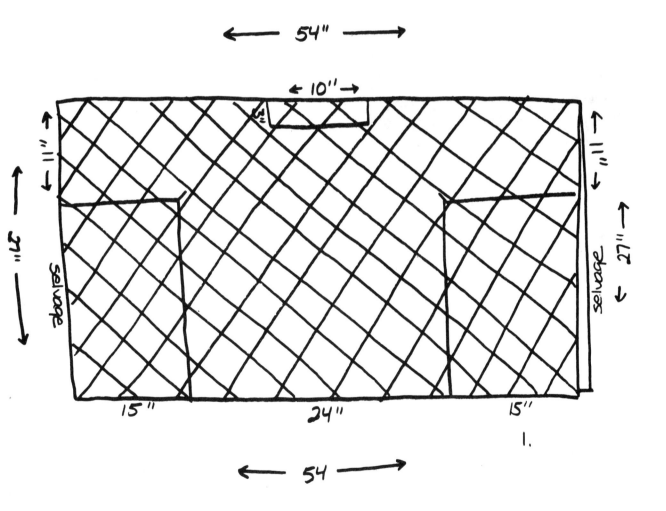

2. Turn under and hemstitch sleeve edges (unless you want to use selvages to finish) and bottom edge. These edges can also be trimmed with velvet or grosgrain ribbon. Use 1" grosgrain ribbon to edge neckline.

Mexican Muslin Blouse

1. This top takes 1 1/2 yards of 36" wide muslin. Measure across body from shoulder to shoulder. Say you measure 16". Add 2" to each shoulder measurement, making total body width measurement 20". (1" for ease; 1" for seam at either shoulder.) Cut away 16" lengthwise, eliminating one selvage. Of course, if width of shoulders measures more than 20" (say 24") you will not cut away as much fabric. Length is 22 1/2" or half of 1 1/2 yards folded.

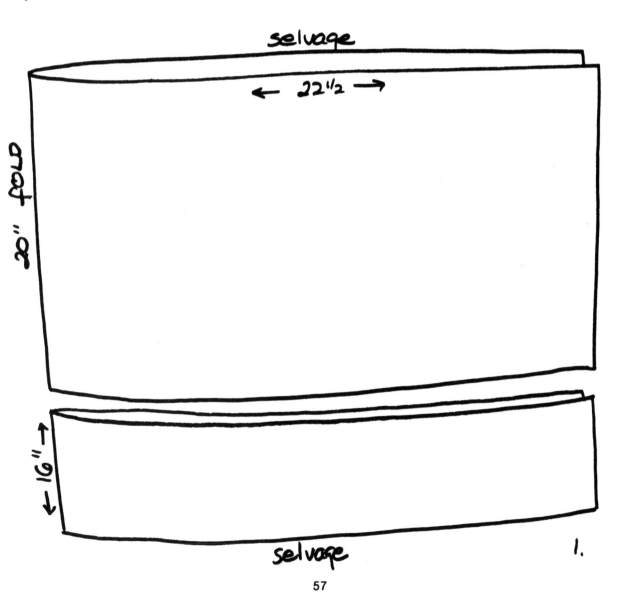

5¹⁄₂"   5¹⁄₂"

7"

3"

7"

22¹⁄₂"

6"

2.

2. Measuring from center front, cut out a rectangular wedge for neckline measuring 3" by 7". Allow 7" (14" around) for armhole and 6" for vent at side. That leaves a seam of 9 1/2" on each side. Hemstitch armholes and vent edges. Edge neckline and bottom with fancy embroidered ribbon.

Hopi Indian Dress

1. Use about three yards of 35" wide fabric so you'll have selvages on both sides. Cut two pieces, both the same size, measuring from shoulder to hem length desired, allowing 2 1/2" for hem. Turn up hem on both pieces of material and machine sew hem while attaching a decorative border to right side. With right sides together, seam in 5" along top edge of fabric on either right or left side, depending on which shoulder you want bare. Seam down the other side, beginning 8" from shoulder seam, to about one foot above finished hem, for a deep slit.

2. Turn garment right side out. Perhaps sew another decorative border above one that is attached to hemline. Tuck under open side (as illustrated with broken line) to bare one shoulder. Use a colorful sash to pull together open selvage sides and secure garment to body. Optional: Use bright thread to make blanket stitch around armhole. (See Hand Stitches, pp. 5-8.)

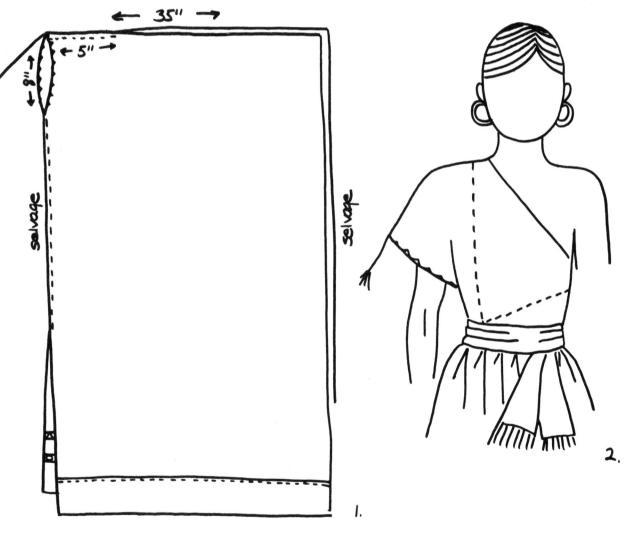

Egyptian Aba

1. Wool challis, crepe, or jersey is nice to make an aba cum hostess gown. Terry cloth is also terrific. Sew together, allowing for a 1/2" seam through center, two pieces of cloth 32" x 95". You now have "one" piece of cloth measuring 62" x 95". Fold cloth with right sides together—the back piece being 50" and the front piece being 45". Cut a piece of fabric (the same used for the aba or a contrasting fabric) measuring 2" wide and 10" down the inside of V and 12" down outside of V for your neckline facing. At top front edge, measure in 19" from fold and cut down 10" in a V-shape (same as facing) for front opening. The top of the opening should be 7" across. Stitch facing in place (see Facts A-Z, p. 15). Clip seam at point of V. Turn under and machine stitch or pink raw facing edge. Make a 4" seam on right and left side of neck opening, leaving 15" on either end of dress for arms to pass through. (On left, the back piece will extend 20" and the front 15".) Hemstitch raw armhole edges in 1". Hem bottom of dress with 2 1/2" hem. Use a 62" strip of fringe for each open edge. Stitch in place with running stitch by hand or machine stitch. If you use fringe on back only, hemstitch front edge.

2. Head goes through 7" opening, 4" seams sit on shoulders, right arm goes through 15" opening at right. Open side drapes down from left shoulder, leaving a breezy space at left. Modest ladies can pin the drape in place at strategic points.

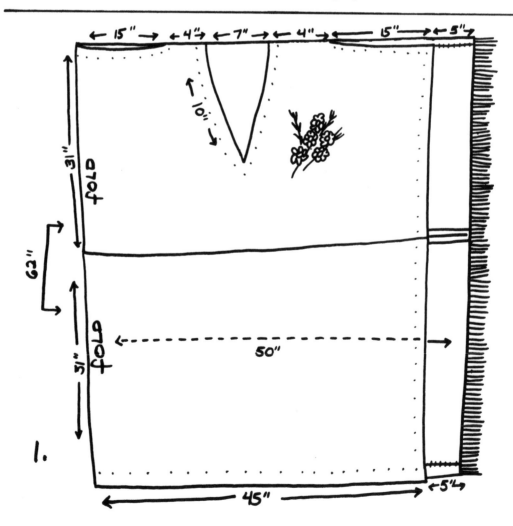

2.

The Big Indian Bedspread Dress

Pay a visit to your local East Indian shop and pick out a really beautiful double bedspread. Most double spreads have a seam lengthwise down the center of the cloth.

1. Open the seam about 15" right in the center, reinforcing the stitching before the entire seam ravels loose. If there isn't a seam, make a 15" slash in the bedspread's middle. Hemstitch the slash.

2. Fold the spread widthwise and stitch the edges leaving room enough to stick your hands through easily.

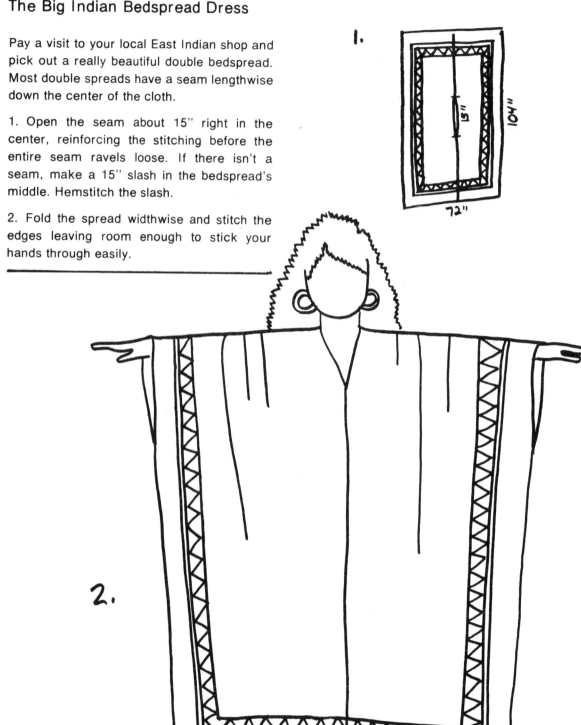

2.

Indian Bedspread Caftan

Use a double Indian print bedspread, standard measurement 104" x 72" (or 3 1/2 yards of 54" wide fabric). Use an overall print that can be easily matched up on seam edges.

Pattern is drawn as it would be laid out on bedspread (Figure 1). For clarification,

pieces have been illustrated as they would look when cut (figures 1a and 1b). There is one back piece (cut on the fold) and two front pieces, making a total of three pieces. Refer to figures 1, 1a, and 1b when cutting out your pattern.

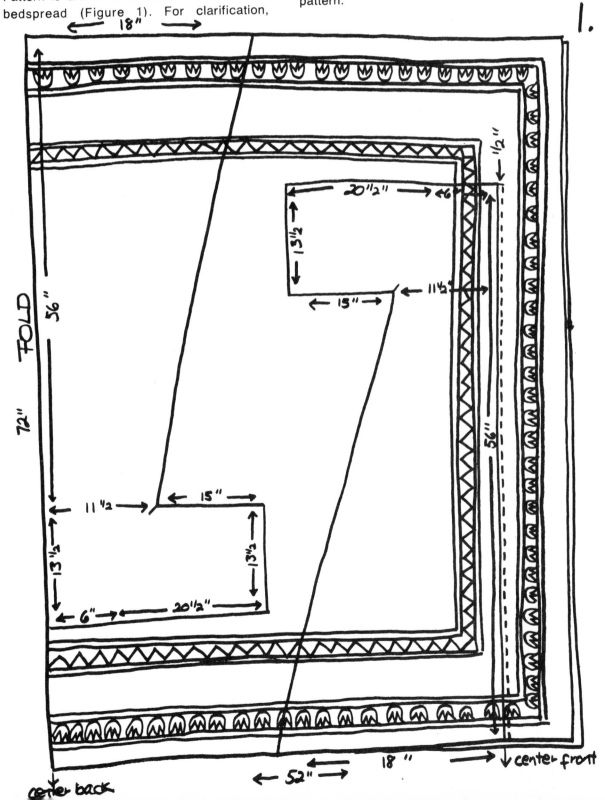

1. Bedspread measures 72" x 104". Fold widthwise right side out so that you form a rectangle 52" wide by 72" long. (If using yardage fold 3 1/2 yards lengthwise, cutting front and back double, one below the other. Center back is on fold.) Once folded be sure edges are even, so borders will match when caftan pieces are sewn together.

For caftan front measure up along right-hand side to your exact length (from shoulder to floor). If you are 5'8" tall, you'll measure 56". This is the standard that is used here. Mark the exact center of border pattern at open ends opposite fold. Add 1/2" for seam allowance to the right of center. (Indicated by broken line.) Use a pencil or chalk and yardstick to mark this line. Cut along this line. This leaves exactly 1/2 of bedspread border plus 1/2" seam allowance. This will make a full border pattern when two front pieces are sewn together. Cutoff border edge can be sewn into a sash if you wish. (I prefer to wear my caftan unsashed.) Along bottom edge measure 18" straight across to the left from center front. Mark this point with pencil. At top of 56" center front line (or whatever your length measurement), measure to the left from center 6" and mark. This is neck opening to fit a head no larger than 22". If head is larger than 22", extend this line as far as needed. Extend 6" line straight across to the left another 20 1/2" and mark with pencil. Measure 13 1/2" straight down from this point (mark a dot with pencil) and 15" in toward center front to make shape of sleeve (mark a dot). Measurement will be 11 1/2" across from underarm dot to center front. Using your yardstick, measure from underarm dot to point where bottom edge extends 18" from center front.

For back, use fold as center back. Top border is used for hem edge of caftan back. Measure and mark (with dots and using yardstick to make straight lines) exactly as you did for the caftan front.

64

Cut out along lines (as shown in Figure 1). You'll have three pieces (two front pieces, one back). With right sides together, stitch shoulder seams. Stitch center front seam. Stitch underarm seams and down side seams. Clip underarm seams at corners.

2. Hemstitch sleeve edges. Use bedspread selvages for hem finishing or hemstitch up 2 1/2".

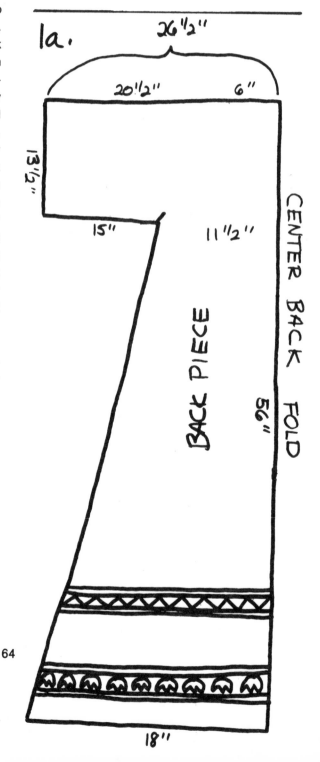

1a.

1b.

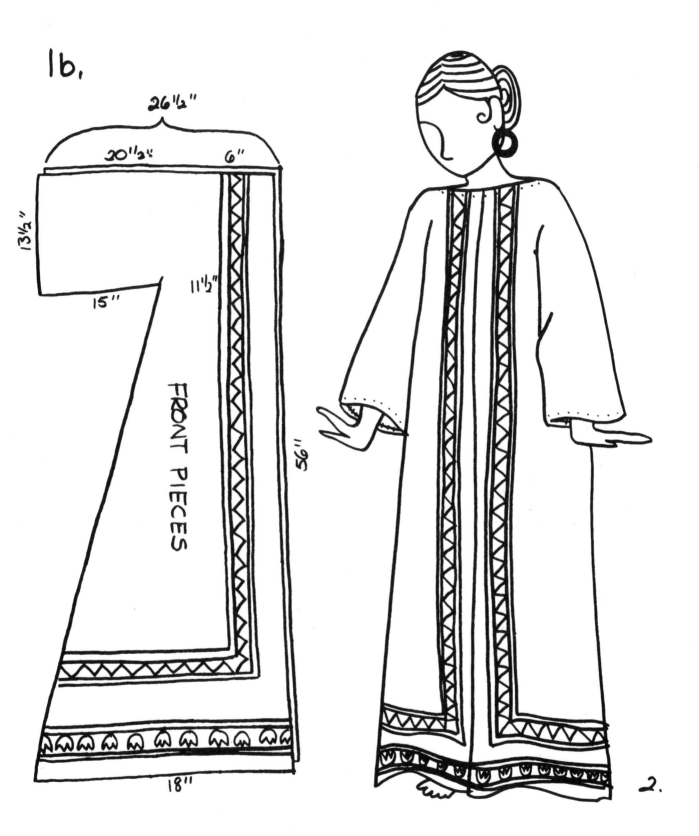

26½"

20¾"   6"

13½"

15"   11½"

FRONT PIECES

56"

18"

2.

8. The Geometric Principle

Many folk cultures made their clothes on the "geometric principle" simply because it "saved on fabric." Cutting on the straight, however, not only saves money but also saves time. It is much quicker and simpler to sew straight pieces together than curved ones.

Often Hispanic, Eastern, and Middle Eastern Cultures carried the "geometric principle" to a sophisticated degree, intricately piecing together strips of cloth under the sleeve, down each side of the garment, at the shoulder and neckline, to shape a garment without curves or darts, merely by sticking to straight seams. I chose to remain with the more simple geometric structures as the purpose of this book is instant construction. But, for inveterate as well as newly curious sewers I recommend the delight of looking through books of national clothes of various countries, particularly the Hispanic, Eastern, and Middle

Eastern ones, to see the artistry in these geometric constructions.

Almost any square, rectangle, triangle, or circle can be made into a garment by cutting or leaving holes through which you can fit your head, arms, or legs. Often, the geometric shape or shapes are molded to your body with elastics, drawstrings, or sashes. But, usually the garment is left hanging loose, the pattern of the fabric or its natural folds as it falls on your body giving it its "personality."

The patterns in this section are broken down into four types: squares, rectangles, triangles, and circles. For the most part, the garments are constructed with square or rectangular shapes. Three garments are made with triangles. There are four designs made with circular shapes.

So we begin with squares.

The John Wayne Skirt

This skirt was made with nine red bandannas, just like the ones cowboys wear around their necks in the movies. Brings to mind John Wayne, of course.

1. The bandannas are usually 15" square. Stitch four of them together to make a 30" square for the skirt front. Stitch four together to make the skirt back, leaving an 8" opening at top of center back. The remaining square will be used for waistband tie. Cut this remaining scarf into three equal strips, each one 5" x 15". Seam these three pieces together to make a waistband tie 45" long. Press open seams.

2. Stitch side seams and press all seams open. Gather top of skirt (see Hand Stitches, pp. 5-8). Pull gathers in to 1" larger than waist measurement to allow for overlap at center back. Now, find center of waistband tie and place at center front. With right sides together, pin waistband tie to skirt (1/2" seam). Bring waistband tie to inside of skirt and baste. Finished waistband tie will be about 2 1/2" wide. Press band. Press extending ends of tie, turning under a 1/2" seam. Now topstitch band (by machine or hand) from one end to the other. When you stitch the band where it is connected to the skirt top, make sure that you catch the band at the right and wrong side with your stitching.

1.

2.

Four Square Dance Dress

1. Buy four 26" square scarves. They can be all one color or the same pattern in different colors. The scarves can also be different patterns and colors if you're daring and have a good eye for jumbling prints and hues. With right sides together, sew two sets of scarves together to make two rectangles. Again, with right sides together, sew the two rectangles to make a dress. Seam in 7" from the top corner to make shoulder line. This leaves a 12" opening for neck. Leave 8" (16" circumference) for armholes. Then sew sides of rectangles down to a spot 12" above lower edge. The 12" is left open for vents on either side of dress.

2. Sash dress with a long rectangular scarf.

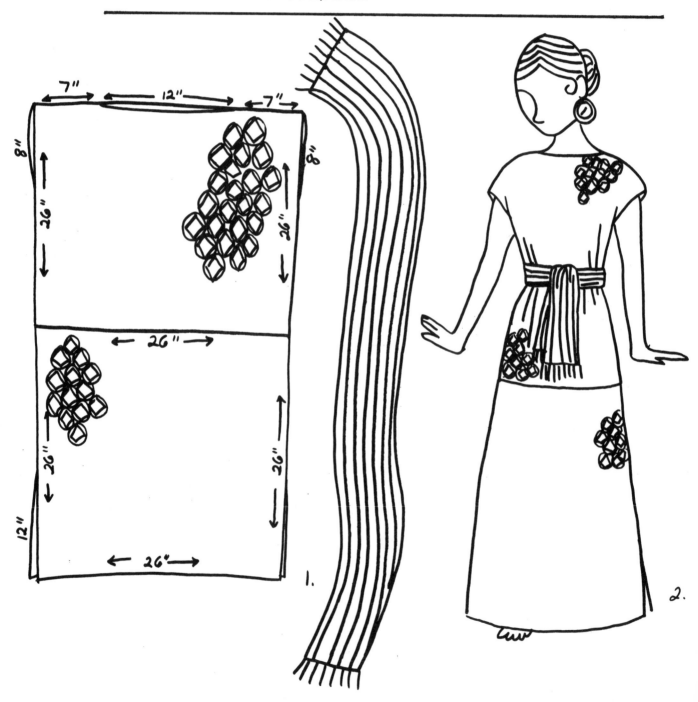

Square Yard Poncho

1. Buy a square of 54" wool. Fringe raw edges 3" deep, or sew on wool fringe. Cut a slash from one corner of square to the center. Hem the raw edges or bind them with grosgrain ribbon or seam tape.

2. Wear over jeans, or anything.

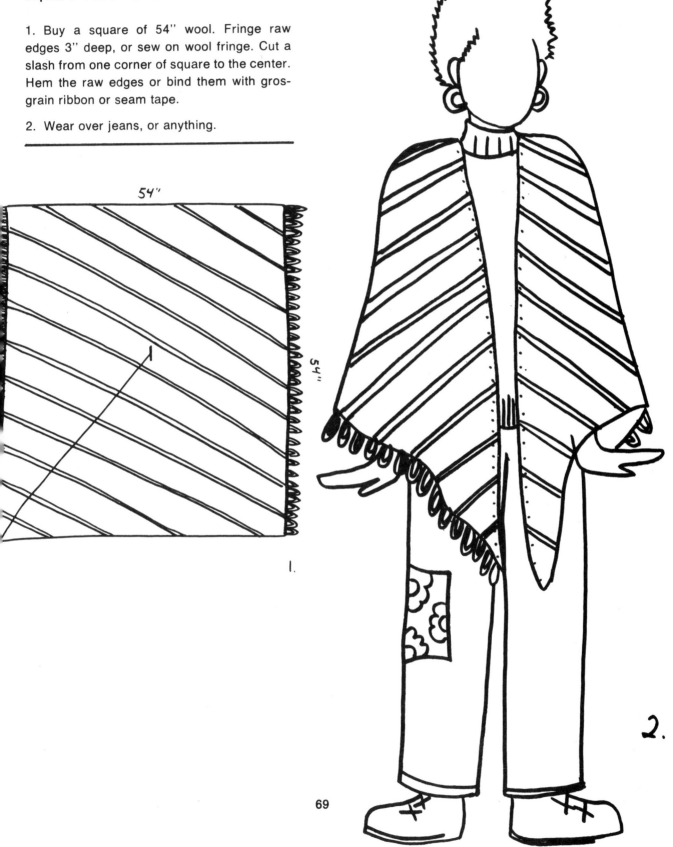

54"

54"

1.

2.

Aunt Myrtle's Square Scarf Top

1. Use a 50" square scarf or a piece of silk cloth the same measurement. Fold scarf (or cloth) in half twice, like a napkin, to find center. Mark center. Unfold scarf and cut a slash 8" on either side from center, making an opening for head that measures 16".

2. On wrong side of fabric hemstitch raw edge of slash (or edge it with bias tape or ribbon). With scarf folded in half, allow 14" (28" around) on each side for armhole. Then make a seam that is 9" long under each armhole. If your body's circumference is too large for the 9" side seam you may want to make it shorter. The scarf top narrows inward the longer the seam gets. It would be possible to make the seam 4" to 5", leaving a nice sexy bare spot on each side.

3. Points of scarf hang at center front and back over pants or skirt. Sleeve points reach anywhere from forearm to wrist, depending upon the length of your arm.

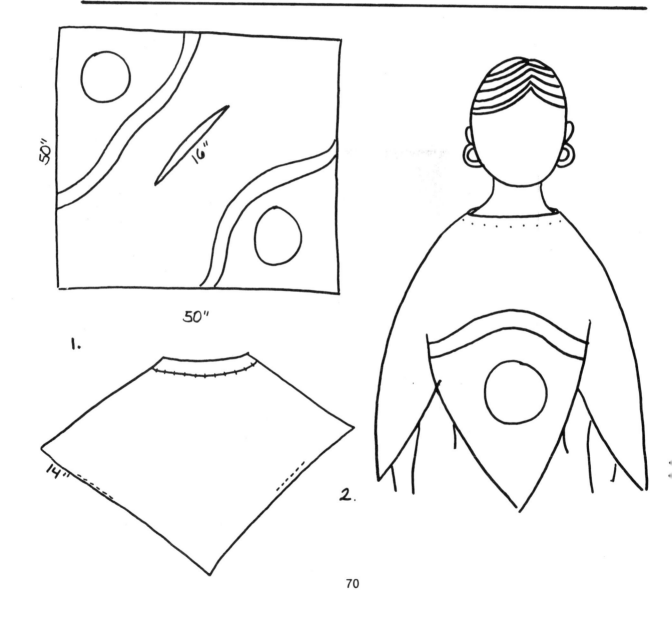

70

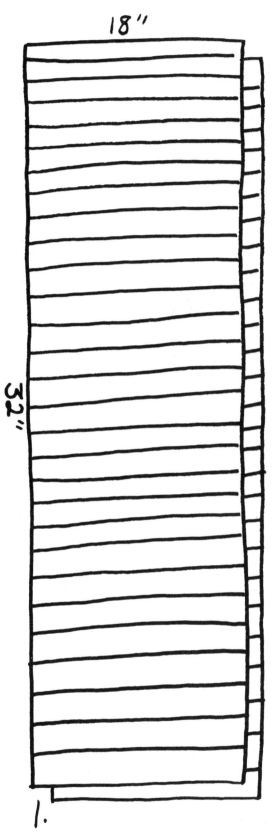

18"

32"

1.

The Poncho from San Pablito

1. The traditional poncho (originating in San Pablito, Mexico) is made with two rectangular strips of cloth measuring 18" x 32", usually woven on a loom so that edges are finished. If your edges are raw, finish with bias tape or ribbon.

2. Each strip is folded in half. One fits into the other, as in Figure 2. First match AB section of each strip and stitch from point A to point B. Then match CD section and stitch from point C to point D. If needed, now sew on edging.

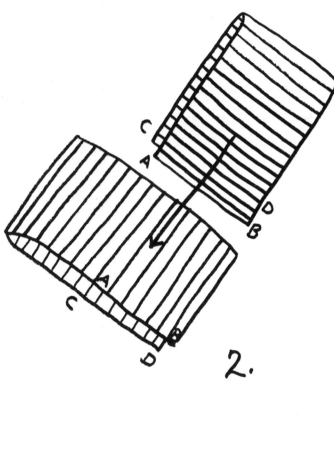

2.

3. Attach a tassel to center front point.

3.

Mexican Huipil

This huipil is made with six rectangles, each 14" wide and 60" long. Huipil means three. Originally these dresses were made of three long pieces of cloth, usually standardized to one size because of the loom width customarily used. Since its origin, however, the huipil, although retaining its name, has been made up in six pieces (this when there are seams on the shoulder). And, it has been made in two pieces and double that in four when there are seams on the shoulders.

1. For this particular huipil, two of the rectangles, the ones used for center front and back, are in fabrics contrasting in color and pattern.

To cut out rectangular neckline, find exact middle of two center pieces (front and back) by folding them lengthwise. Measure down 3" from fold and lightly mark with pencil. Measure over 5" from fold along top edge and mark. Measure down 3" from top edge and mark at this point. Use a small ruler and lightly connect lines to form a rectangle. Cut out rectangular area, which will measure 10" x 3" when center pieces are unfolded.

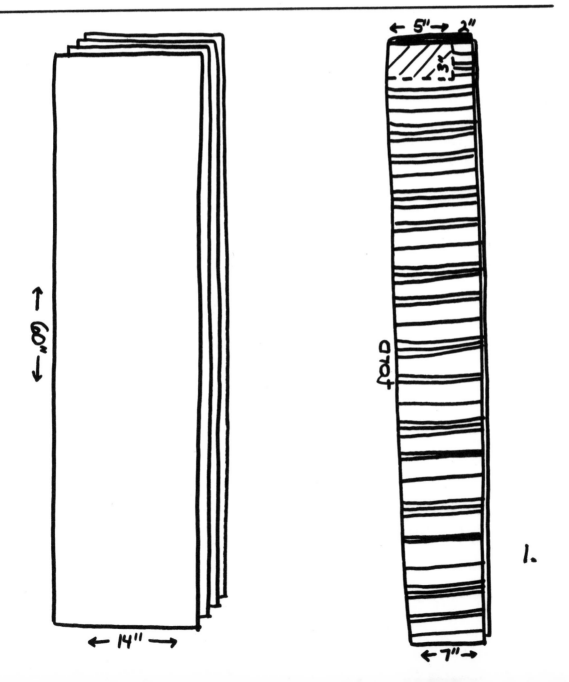

2. Edge rectangular neck areas on both center pieces with grosgrain ribbon. With right sides of fabric together, seam a rectangle to either side of center front and center back panel. Press open seams. Right sides together, seam front and back of huipil at shoulder and at sides, leaving a 14" (28" in circumference) opening for armhole.

3. Hemstitch armhole and hem. Optional: Sew grosgrain ribbon along seams front and back and on either side of armhole and side seam.

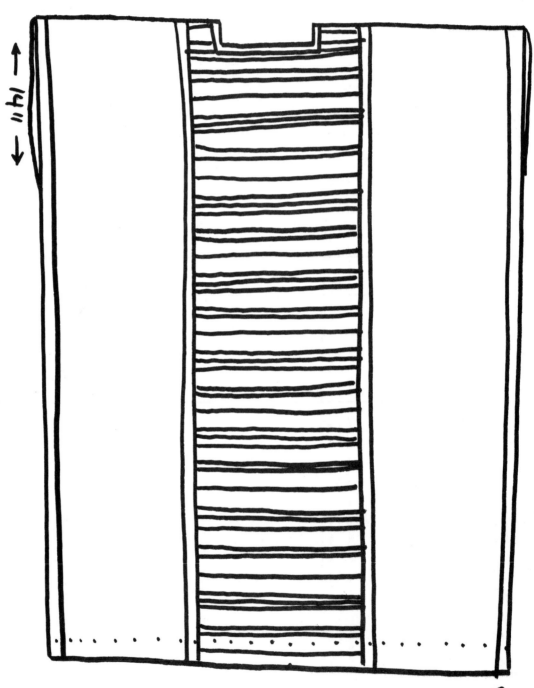

14"

2.

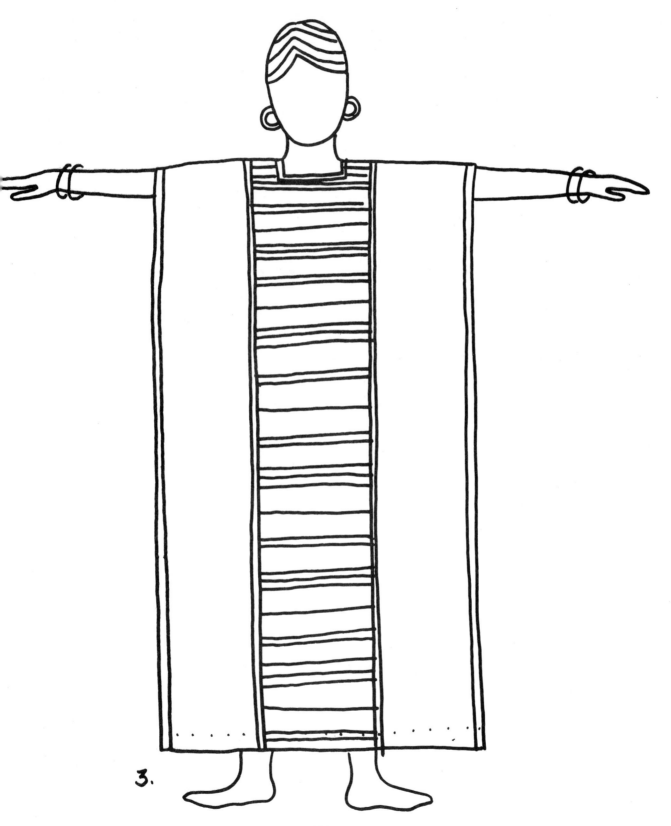

3.

Oaxaca Huipil

The huipil dates back to the time of Cortez. This particular huipil originated in Oaxaca where it was made of two long pieces of fabric 74" long by 21" wide (the width of the loom).

1. This huipil can be made with two long pieces of cloth or four as demonstrated here. Either way, you would measure from shoulder to length desired, allowing for a 2 1/2" hemline, to get accurate measurement for rectangles. Width used is the original 21".

2. Right sides together, seam two rectangles to make dress front and two to make dress back. Leave a 9" opening on the end of each seam. This will be the neck opening. Seam two joined front and two joined back rectangles at top and down sides, leaving a 12" (24" circumference) opening for arms. Hemstitch around armholes, at neckline, and hemline.

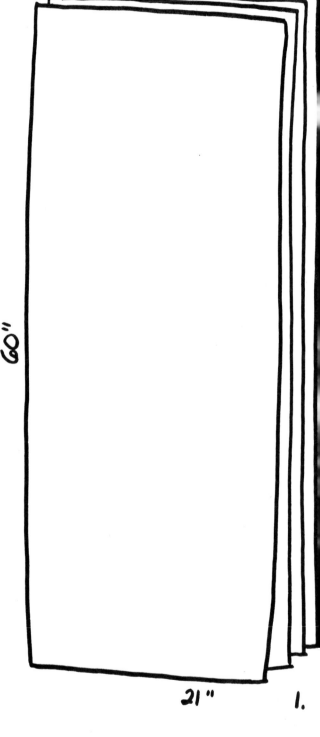

60"

21"   1.

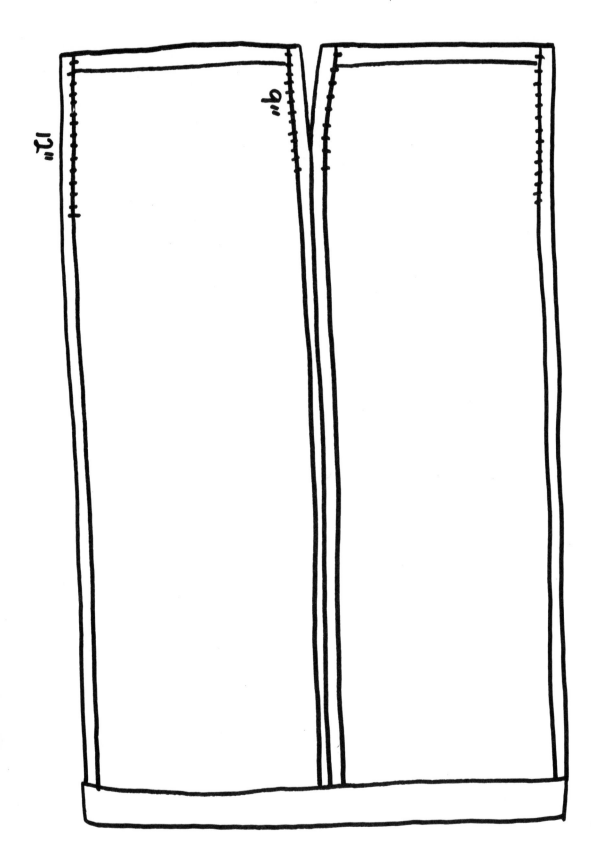

3. Sew a decorative braided cord at center
front of dress.

3.

Eight Rectangle Egyptian Aba

This particular aba is strictly ceremonial. It is not worn much today as it's too elaborate. It's the sort of thing worn when a neighboring sheik comes to visit.

1. Four rectangles 25" x 29" make up the aba's back, four rectangles 25" x 26" make up the front. For back, with right sides together, sew two sets of rectangles along 25" side. Press open seam. Now you'll have two large rectangles 25" x 57". With the right sides together, seam them along 57" side.

For the front, with the right sides together, seam the rectangles along the 25" side. Press with right sides facing forward and facing each other, hemstitch 1/2" under on left and right of front center.

Right sides together, match up front pieces to back piece at outside edges, leaving a front space 6" wide. Stitch at shoulder line. For armhole allow 14" down on each side (28" circumference). Then stitch garment from this point down sides to hem. Hemstitch bottom edge.

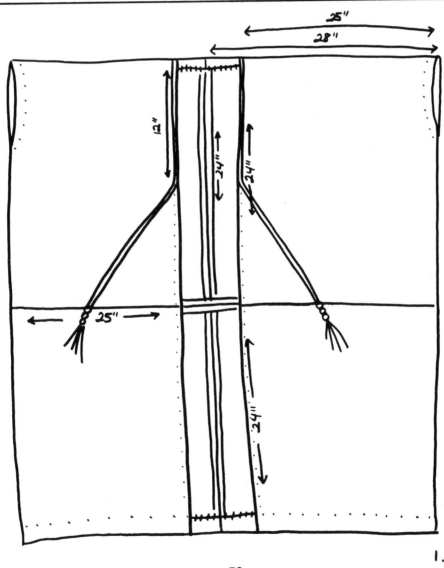

I.

79

2. Stitch a braid or ribbon 12'' down center
left and right of center front to make a tie
closure for aba.

2.

Guatemalan Rectangle Dress

This dress, made with eight rectangles, originated in the Chichicas Terango section of Guatemala. For good measure, make this up in muslin first to see if it fits accurately. You may like the muslin so much you'll leave the dress in that fabric.

1. Four rectangles make up central body of dress. For 36" hips add 20" to measurement, bringing the total to 56". This divided into four makes four rectangles 14" wide (this includes 1/2" seam allowances at sides and front, which will bring the width around hips when dress is sewn to 53"). As a general rule, allow yourself 20" more than your hip measurement

to start. You can whittle down the size of the rectangles if this proves too ample for you. This makes up into a loosely fitted garment if your bosom and shoulders aren't too far out of proportion with hip measurement. For length measure from shoulder to desired hemline, allowing for 2 1/2" hem.

2. Right sides together, seam two rectangles together lengthwise, leaving 5" open at one end, 6" on the other. The first opening will be at the neckline, the second will be a skirt vent. Hemstitch openings. Right sides together, seam remaining two rectangles from top to bottom for back.

3. Right sides together sew back and front shoulder seam in 7" from outer edge in direction of illustrated arrow.

4. Gather area that remains unseamed: front 7" space from neckline opening to mid-shoulder around back of neckline to shoulder midpoint around again to other front shoulder opening. Shoulder areas on either side of neckline opening gather into 3 1/2". Back of neck area gathers into 7", or 3 1/2" on either side of center back seam. This brings total neck size to 14". Neckline opening will spread apart in front to accommodate any additional room needed around neck. A piece of fabric 15" long, 3" wide is needed for neckband, which will be sewn around gathered area. Hemstitch back a 1/2" seam on either end of neckband. Iron under a 1/2" seam on one side. Right sides together, seam unironed side of neckband to gathered neckline. Turn ironed seam allowance against gathering on inside of dress and hemstitch. Blindstitch outer 1" edge of neckline on either side of neck opening.

5. Each sleeve is composed of two rectangles. Measure from bicep to wrist for length of rectangles that will make up sleeves. (Here 14" is used as standard length.) On the average woman, seam where sleeve attaches to dress will reach to bicep. Measure circumference of biceps. Add 6" to that measurement. Two inches will be taken up with seams (1/2" on either side of each rectangle). Here 16" is used for standard bicep circumference, half of that, 8", for rectangle's width. Seam rectangles on one side. Press seams flat. Turn rectangles to right side.

6. Match right side of sleeve seams to right side of shoulder seams. Seam dress and sleeve together at outer raw edges.

7. Turn dress to wrong side. Leaving an 8" vent at bottom, seam dress up each side. Make a right corner at armhole point A and continue seam out to wrist. Press open seams.

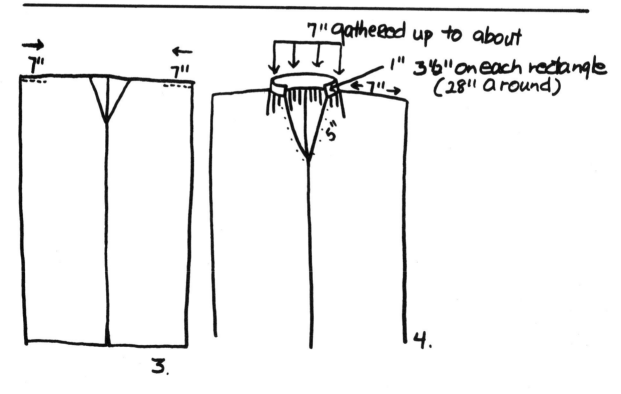

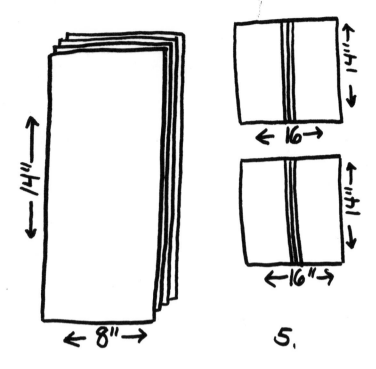

14"

8"

16

16"

5.

6.

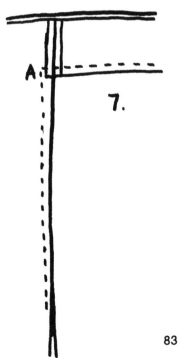

A

7.

8. Turn dress to right side. Gather sleeve around wrist, allowing 2" more than wrist circumference for freedom of movement. Wristband will measure 3" wide by circumference of your wrist, plus 2" for ease. (9" is used here, allowing for 1/2" seam on each end.) Seam two ends together to make a circle. Press circle to make a fold as with neckband. Press a 1/2" seam up around one raw edge. Attach unironed edge to gathered sleeve, right sides together as with neckband. Hemstitch ironed-up edge on inside of sleeve.

9. Finish dress with standard 2 1/2" hem.

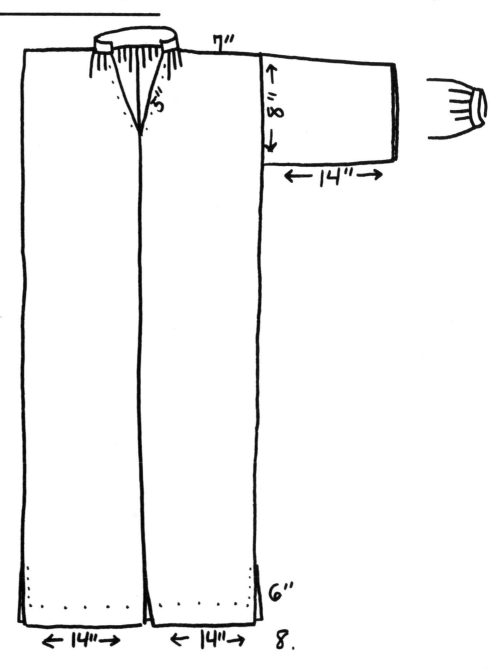

9.

Guatemalan Shirt
for Men or Women

This shirt from the Todos Santos district of Guatemala works on a similar principle to the eight rectangle dress. If the wearer's shoulders are not extraordinarily wide, and numerical figures are followed accurately (starting with your chest measurement), this shirt can be made to fit any size. Here the figures are established for a size 12. As with the eight rectangle dress, this shirt should first be sewn up in muslin to test size. Adjustments in size can be made in width of central and sleeve rectangles. Usually neck is large enough to fit all sizes. This shirt can also be lengthened to make a dress or robe.

1. Four rectangles make up central body of shirt. Four rectangles make up sleeves. For measurement of central rectangles take chest or bust measurement. (Here standard was 36".) Add 22" to that figure. (Total in this instance is 58".) Divide by 4. This gives four rectangles measuring 14 1/2" in width. Measure from shoulder to spot on body where you want shirt to end. Here established measurement was 33 1/2". If you are making a dress or robe this measurement would be longer. For a size 12 shirt, four central rectangles measure 14 1/2 by 33 1/2" in size. The measurement of your rectangles, of course, will depend upon your individual size.

33 ½

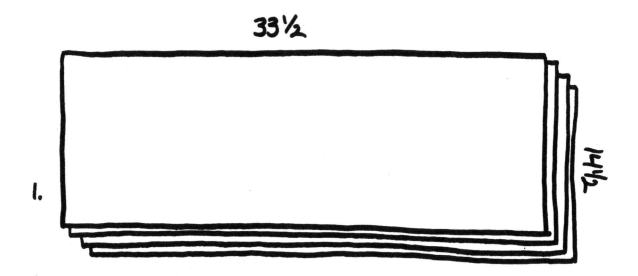

1.

14½

2. Seam two rectangles together lengthwise to make a back piece.

3. Seam two more rectangles together for front piece leaving a 9 1/2" opening on one end. Press open seam. Hemstitch 9 1/2" opening.

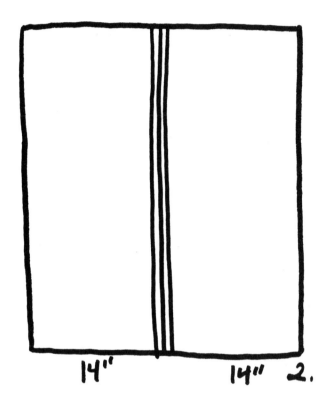

14"   14"   2.

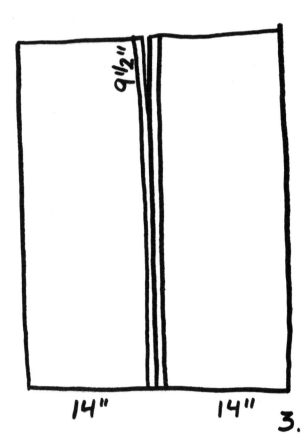

9½"

14"   14"   3.

4. Right sides together, seam front and back pieces at top, 7 1/2" in from outer edge. Press open seams. Turn central body piece to right side.

5. Each sleeve is composed of two rectangles. Dimensions for rectangles are achieved in the following manner. Slip central body piece over head. Note point where shoulder line falls over each shoulder onto each arm. Measure from these points to wrists. Add 1" to this measurement—1/2" for seam allowance to attach rectangles to central body

piece, another 1/2" for seam allowance on sleeve.

6. Standard length used here is 15". So rectangle will measure 15" in length. Measure arm's circumference. (Here standard for size 12 is 11".) Add 2" to the 11" for four seam allowances of 1/2" each. Add 15" for ease. (Here total measurement is 28".) Divide this in two. Rectangles will each measure 14" in width. Cut four rectangles (two for each sleeve) 14" x 15".

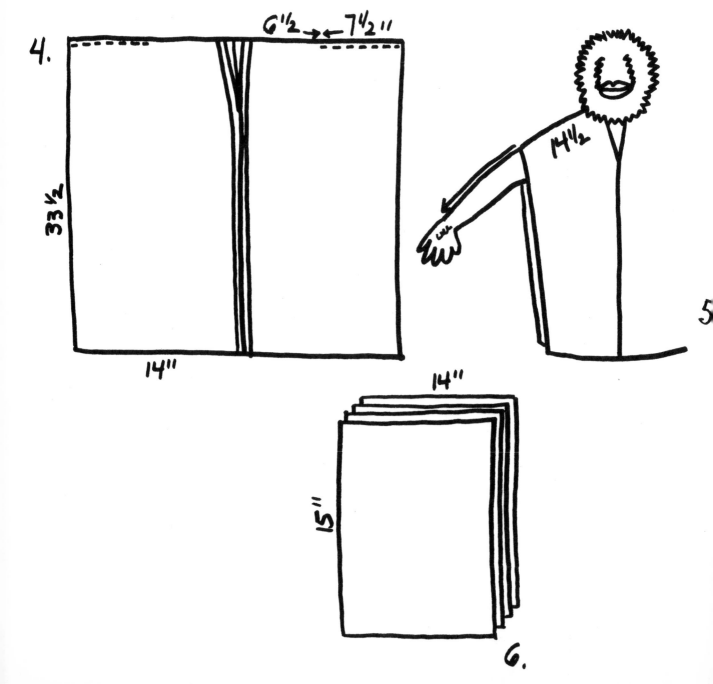

4.

6'½ → ← 7'½"

33½

14"

14½

5

14"

15"

6.

7. Seam two sets of rectangles together lengthwise. Press open seams.

8. Match right side of sleeve seams to right side of shoulder seams. Stitch shoulder rectangles to central body rectangles.

9. Press stitched sleeve rectangles away from central body rectangles.

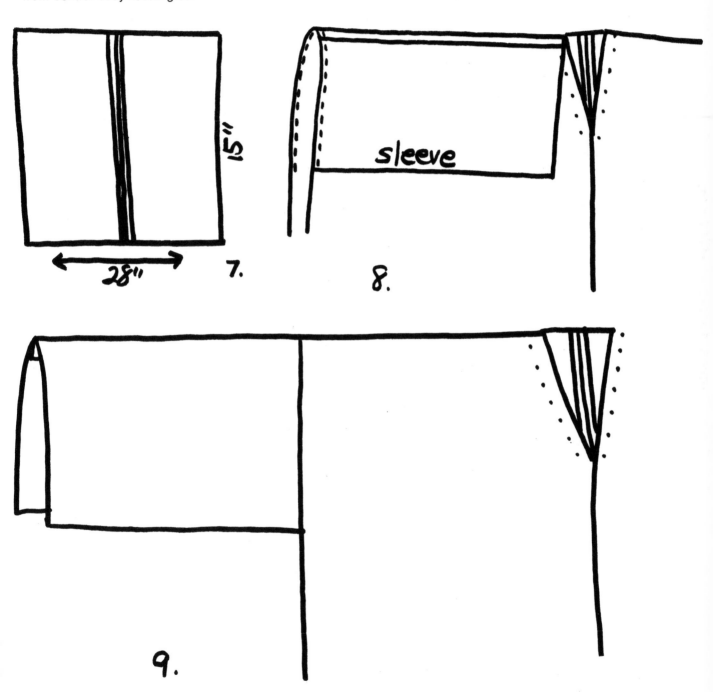

15"

28"

7.

sleeve

8.

9.

10. Turn garment to wrong side. Stitch from end of sleeves to right angles where sleeves of central body rectangles connect. Then continue stitching to bottom edge of garment. Press open seams.

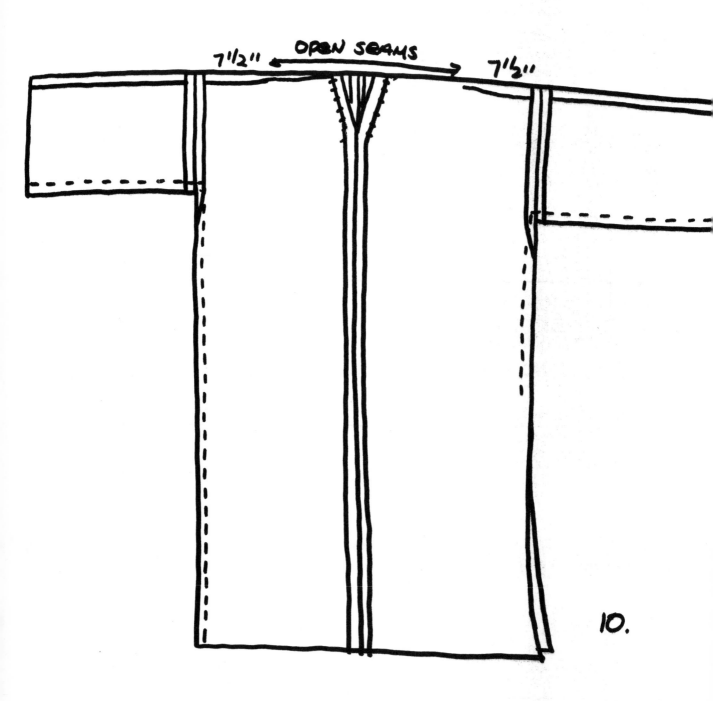

11. Collar will be attached to 28" neck opening (6 1/2" opening on either side of front center seam, 7 1/2" on either side of back center seam). Cut a rectangle for collar measuring 12" x 33"—4" for collar lap, 1" for seam allowance.

12. Fold rectangle lengthwise and seam ends. Then seam 2" in toward center. Press open seams.

13. Turn to right side and press again until right corners are as straight as possible. Press up 1/2" edge all along bottom of rectangle. (One inch has been taken up in side seam, 4" have been seamed along bottom edge.) That leaves a pressed-up opening measuring 28".

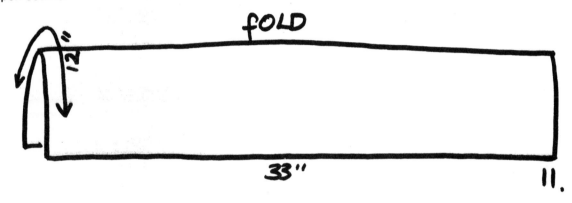

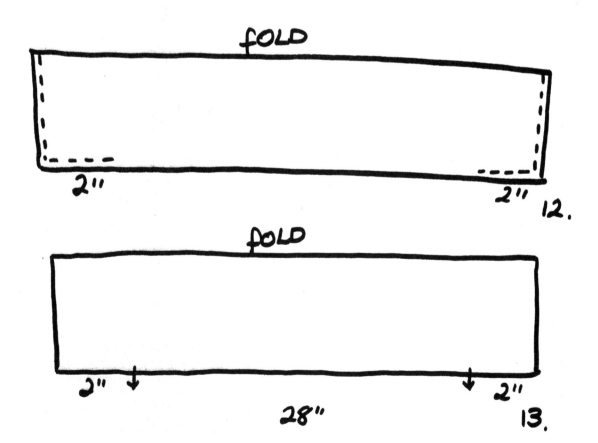

14. Center collar at back seam. Catch shirt up into collar's pressed opening. You will not be able to allow a 1/2" seam but pin up as much fabric as possible to fit into opening without puckering; probably 1/4 to 1/2". Pin shirt inside pressed-up folds of collar from center back seam to center front seam. A lap 2" long should extend over each side. Collar can be folded once, as it is too high to be worn straight up when sewn to shirt. Wear a costume jewelry or ordinary pin at point A so collar will not turn back too far and show 9 1/2" seamed edge. Note: Or attach a button and elastic loop. (See One-Seam Button-up Skirt, p. 43.)

15. Hemstitch sleeve edges and bottom edges of shirt.

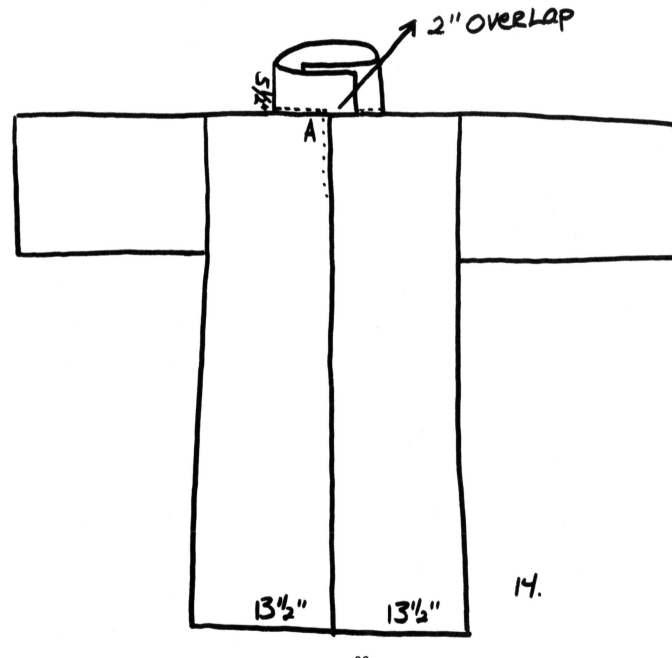

92

15.

Aunt Myrt's Caftan

This is the caftan Aunt Myrtle made from five towels.

1. Each towel measures 24" x 46": four towels are used for skirt, one for bodice.

2. With right sides together seam two towels together lengthwise. Now you have two sets of seamed towels. Measure circumference of ribcage at area underneath bosom. Say measurement is 31". Add 10" to that figure for ease, another 1" for seam allowance. Measurement is now 42". Divide that by 2, measurement is 21". Gather each of two sets of seamed towels 21" along top edge. Fifth towel is folded lengthwise, then widthwise to find center. From center point slash towel out 8" on either side. Hemstitch opening. Right sides together match center edge of one side of bodice to center edge of one side of skirt. Stitch right sides together. Repeat with other side of bodice and of skirt.

1.

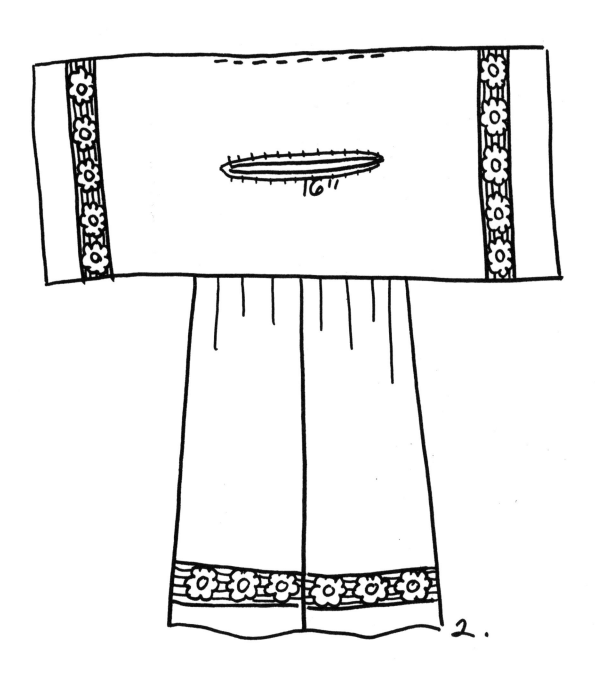

16"

2.

3. Turn stitched garment to wrong side. Stitch from end of sleeves to right angle under arm down to hemline.

4. Turn garment to right side.

18"

3.

4.

Algerian Pants

The Algerian pants are probably best made up in soft fabric, like voile or jersey, so all that fullness doesn't make them too bulky to wear. Wear them for dancing, walking, anything.

1. Cut two rectangles measuring 26" x 24" and two squares measuring 25" x 25".

2. Right sides together, attach squares to rectangles so you get the shape shown in Figure 2. Numbers have been adjusted to account for inches of fabric taken up in seams and/or hems. Press. Leave two 6" openings on either side of rectangle designated for front. Hemstitch openings. At bottom edge, seam in from point A to point B, leaving "legholes" on either side. Press. (To get measurement of leghole, measure circumference of knee at point under knee. Circumference used here is 14". Areas from outer edges to points A or B will measure half of that, or 7".)

3. For major part of waistband, cut a rectangle that measures 3/4 of your total waist circumference, plus 1" for seam allowances. Width of the waistband is 7", 1" of that allowed for seams. For front of waistband cut a rectangle measuring 1/4 of waist circumference. Add 2" for overlap onto major part of waistband. Add another 1" for seam allowances. Fold both parts of waistband lengthwise. Press. Press in 1/2" seams on ends of major part of waistband. Them hemstitch these seams. Press up a 1/2" seam around bottom edges of both major and front waistband parts. Press in a 1/2" seam on side edges of front waistband part. Insert two 6 1/2" ribbons 1/2" into each side of front part of waistband. Pin ribbons in place. To permanently attach ribbons topstitch 1/2" in along front edge. Hand stitch through both layers of fabric, with tacking stitch, two 6 1/2" ribbons 2 1/2" in from front edges of major waistband part.

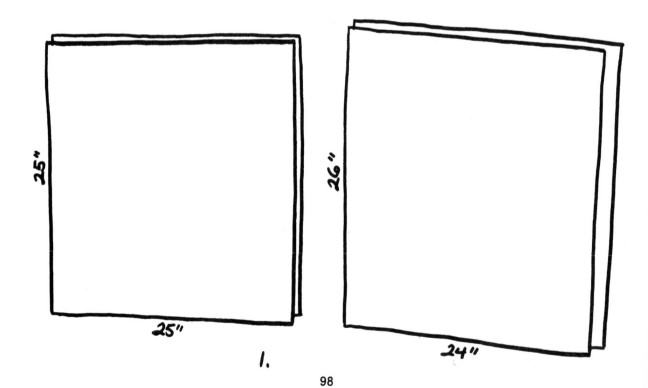

1.

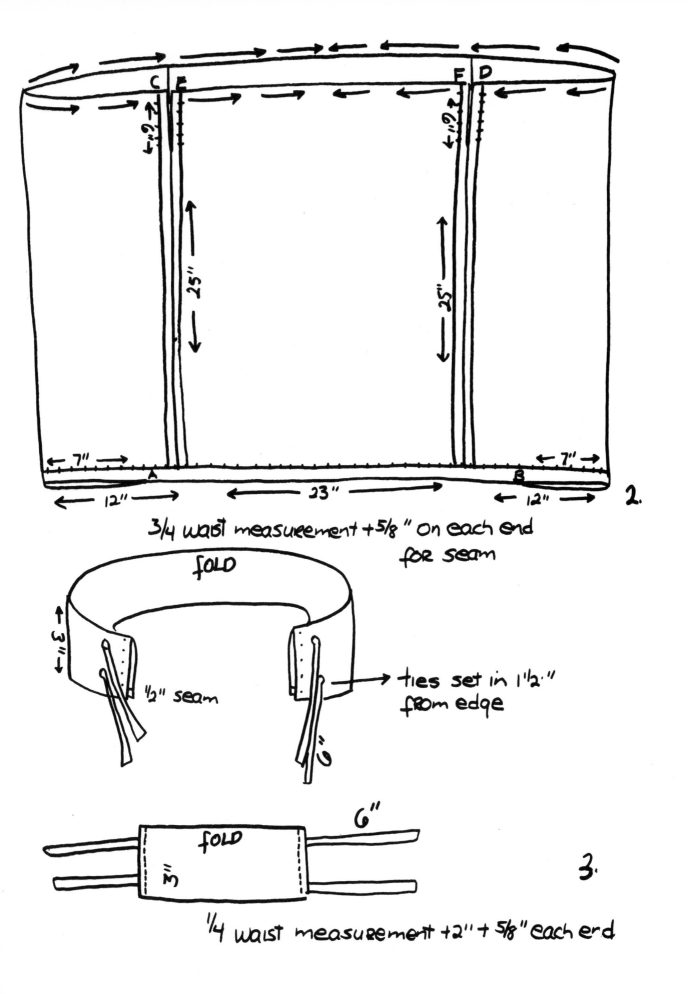

3/4 waist measurement + 5/8" on each end for seam

2.

fold

3"

1/2" seam

ties set in 1 1/2" from edge

6"

fold

6"

3"

3.

1/4 waist measurement + 2" + 5/8" each end

4. With wrong side of fabric out fold waistline into pleats going in direction of arrows (Figure 2). Fold pleats as deep or as numerous as need be to fit into major part of waistband from points C to D. Then fold pleats in directions of arrows to fit into front part of waistband from E to F. Place waistbands over pleats from C to D and E to F, with 1/2" pressed-up edges on either side of pleats. Pin to secure. Topstitch waistbands to pleats from C to D and E to F. Ribbons will tie waistband together to hold Algerian pants in place.

A Middle Eastern
Something or Other

Wear this for a robe, a beachcoat, any rompabout.

1. Cut four rectangles, 52 1/2" x 26". Lay four rectangles on the floor, two sets each, wrong sides together facing each other. Mark a spot (A) on top edges 3" left and right of center front. On outer edges, mark a spot (B) 16" down on sides. With a straightedge ruler mark a line from point A to B. Cut away excess fabric at top on all four rectangles. Now mark a spot (C) 6" down at left and right of center front. Draw a line from A to C on both top rectangles. Cut away excess fabric on two front rectangles to make neckline. Don't cut two back rectangles. Turn back 1/2" from A to C on both front rectangles and hemstitch.

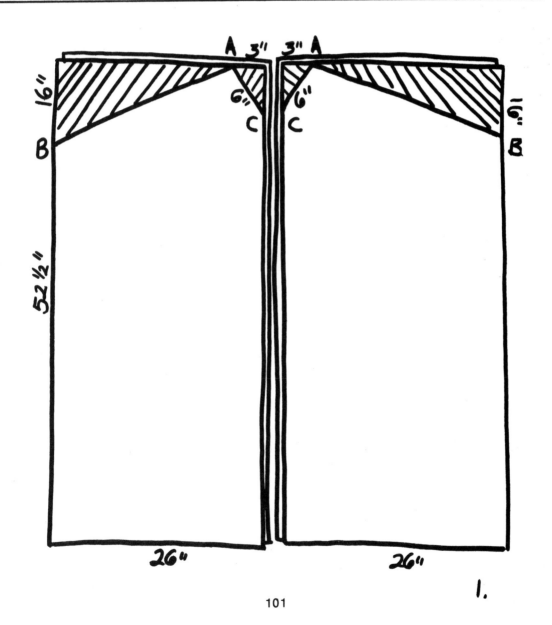

2. Right sides together, seam two front modified rectangles at center front. Right sides together, seam two back modified rectangles at center back. With two sets of seamed rectangles, right sides together, seam from A to B on either side of neckline making shoulder lines. Hemstitch neckline at back from A to A. Finish with standard 2 1/2" hem.

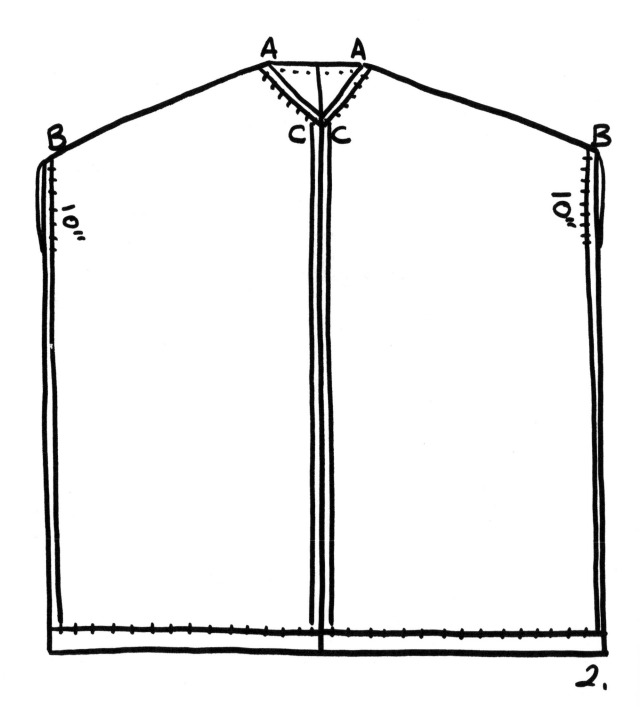

2.

3. Here it is—a Middle Eastern "something or other."

3.

Triangular-Pointed Bandanna Mini

This miniskirt is made with four bandannas sewn "triangle-wise." You could continue to add tiers of bandannas to make a pointed midi skirt.

1. Take four bandannas, with triangular points together, as in illustration. Pin bandannas together on wrong side to hold to make a sample skirt, which you will try on, adjusting pins when necessary. Turn down triangular points (see broken line in illustration) to make a circumference that will fit waistline. Leave opening (see arrow) between two bandannas to make it easy to step into skirt once sewn. Bandannas are sewn together on wrong side to make a pointed skirt.

2. Sew a grosgrain ribbon around skirt's waistline, leaving enough of an overlap so it can tie into an ample sash in back at point of opening.

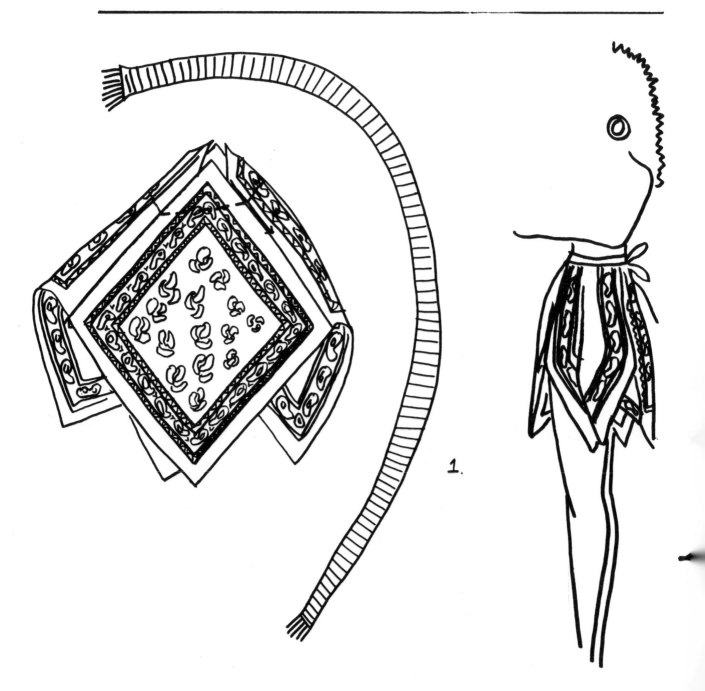

1.

Big Scarf Dress

1. Hold two large scarves, right sides together, so triangular points are facing up. Turn points under 5" at top, stitch 1/2" to 1" down from fold to make a casing through which ties will be drawn (Figure 1). For armhole allowance, measure 15" down from fold. From bottom of armhole allowance on both sides stitch 25" to lower edge of side triangular points. Press seams.

2. Turn garment to right side. Tie drawstrings together over shoulders.

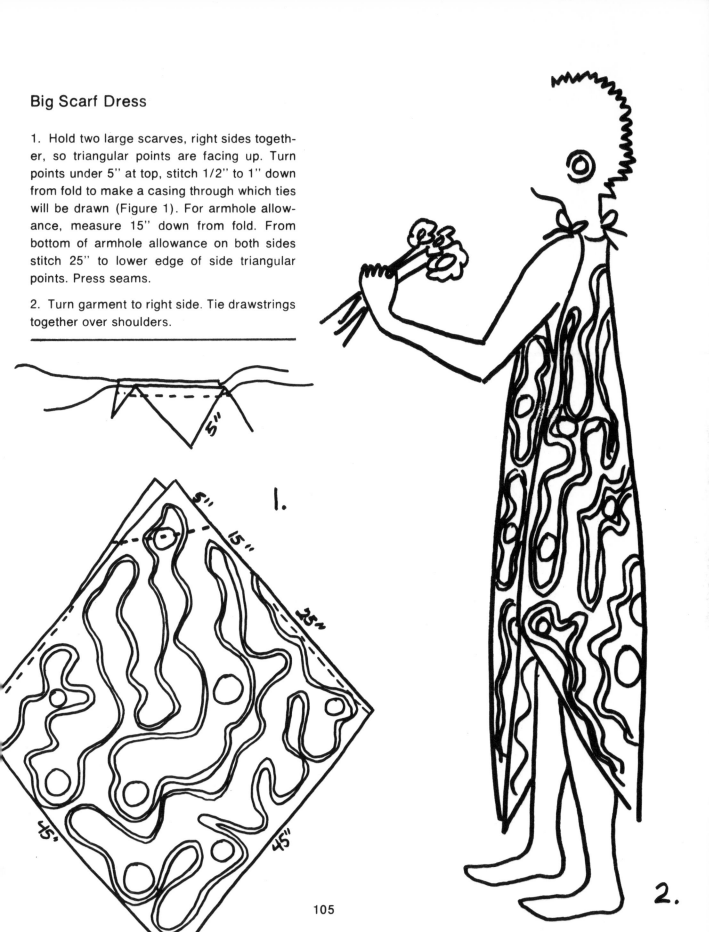

Big, Grand Full-Circle Cape

Made out of heavy wool.

1. This cape takes 4 squares of 60" fabric. Stack them, right sides up, as in Figure 1. Measure the neckhole by finding the right radius (measurement from A to edge of neck circle). Add 2" for ease to your neck measurement. For example, if your neck is 13", add 2" for 15". Divide by 3.14 (or just 3, which I use) for the diameter, 5". Half that, 2 1/2" is the radius. Hold the end of your tape measure at A, follow your correct radius around to mark the arc. Cut along this line. Measure 60" out from A in same way for hemline, and cut away excess fabric.

2. Seam circle pieces together on three sides, leaving one side unseamed for front opening.

3. Bind cape around all edges with ribbon. Bind neckline with ribbon, too, leaving ample amount to make a tie, if you don't attach a hood.

4. To make hood: fold a 20" x 13" piece of fabric widthwise. Make a curve approximating shape on top of rectangle in Figure 4. Begin a curve about 3" down on both top corners of rectangle. Cut away excess material. Seam along raw edges at top of hood. Make tucks on either side of hood. Pin, as you'll readjust these tucks while matching hood up to fit neckline. Press seams. Turn hood to right side. Match center back of hood to center back of cape. Then, with right sides of hood against right side of cape, pin hood and neckline together, adjusting tucks until front of hood matches exactly with front of cape. Bind hood with same ribbon used for cape, leaving enough length to tie.

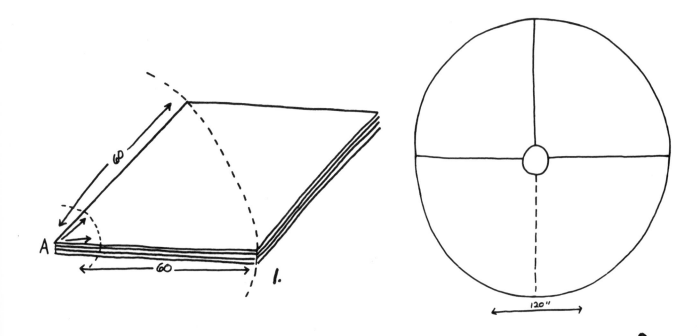

A

60

60

120"

2.

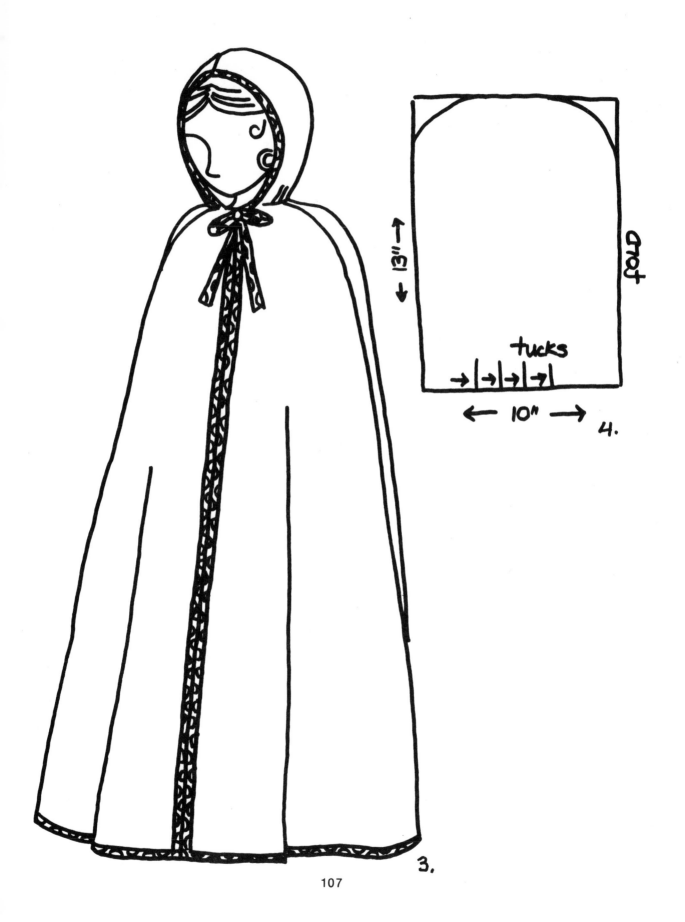

grat

tucks

→|→|→|→|→|

←— 10" —→

3.

4.

City Sandy's Semicircular Skirt

This takes two squares of fabric 45" wide if you want a long skirt, 35" wide for a shorter one. Extra fabric (about another yard 45" square) will be needed for ruffle, although it can be of contrasting material.

1. Fold fabric so that you have a selvage edge at top and bottom. To cut the circular waistline requires a knowledge of simple geometry. First measure your waistline circumference. Say that measurement is 22" (alas, were it!). Divide that figure by 3.14, which is pi (or π in geometric symbology). 7 1/3 is the approximate figure for the diameter, a good enough summation for those of us who are not math whizzes. From fold edge measure over and down 7 1/3. Also measure 7 1/3 from top left corner toward lower right corner. Mark these three points (see Figure 1). Then connect them circularly. Fabric above circular line will be cut away. To get circular skirt length measure 45" (or 35" if this is fabric width used) from top left corner to right-hand corner, using a flexible tape measure or a string. Mark spots along the curved line with a pencil as you move the tape or string from left to right. Then fill in the complete circular line. Cut away excess fabric. To make skirt ruffles cut four strips of fabric (they can be pieced) approximately the length of the circular hem. Seam four strips together to make one large circular strip. Press seam. Machine stitch a 1/4" to 1/2" hem around bottom edge of circular skirt. Begin to gather up ruffle. It can be adjusted to fit when attached to skirt. Right sides together sew semicircle at selvage edge leaving a 6" opening at top. Opening can be left with selvage for finish or can be hemstitched.

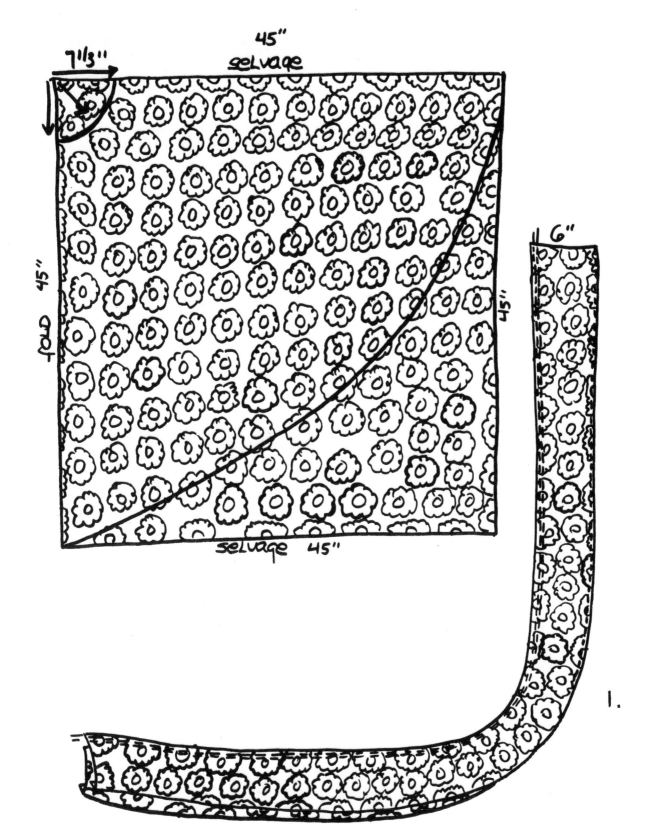

7"/3"

45"
selvage

fold 45"

45"

6"

selvage 45"

1.

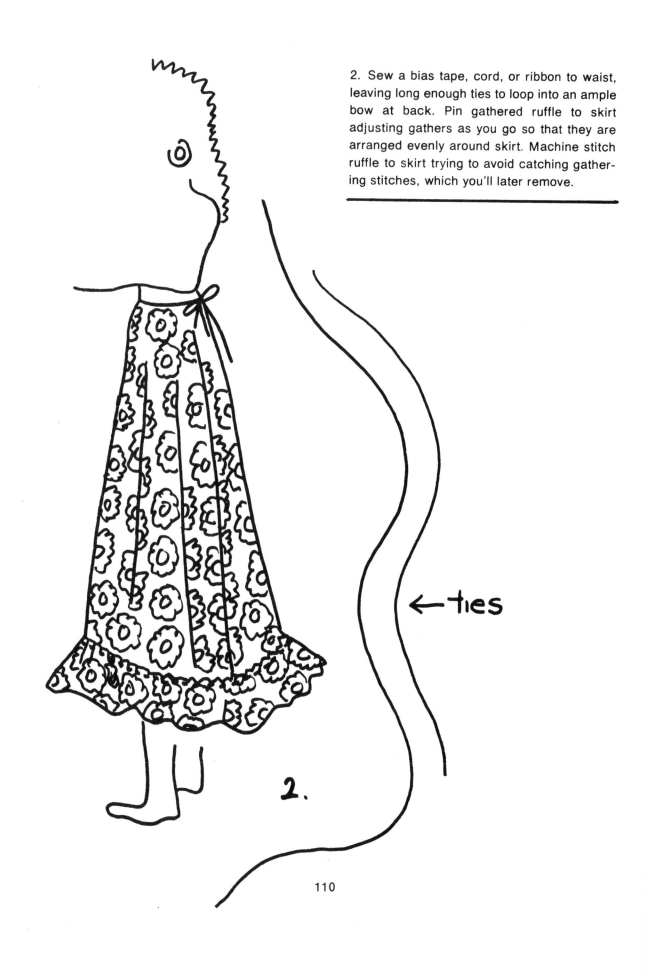

2. Sew a bias tape, cord, or ribbon to waist, leaving long enough ties to loop into an ample bow at back. Pin gathered ruffle to skirt adjusting gathers as you go so that they are arranged evenly around skirt. Machine stitch ruffle to skirt trying to avoid catching gathering stitches, which you'll later remove.

← ties

2.

110

9. Drawstrings and Other Strings Attached

Noticeably missing from this book are darts, gussets, godets, shaped seams, all provoking nuisances. I know, I've used all of these devices and have come back to tell the tale. They are not necessary. They are a bother. On the other hand, if you style yourself after the Duchess of Windsor you'll want to learn to sew darts, gussets, godets, and shaped seams. But, that's another book. This book makes sewing easy for you.

This chapter (in *this* book) tells how to use drawstrings and ties to mold clothes to your body, or even to just hold them on. It couldn't be easier. You'll find that two yards of cloth held together with a couple of ties makes a clever dress (the Fly-by-Night, p. 114), that some lovely material pulled together with a drawstring (the Little Pregnant Number, p. 116) makes a nifty maternity dress. In fact, you'll find that you can tie a bikini—and a lot of other garments—on in no time flat.

Argentinean Chiripa

Gauchos on the pampas wear their chiripas over riding pants. They are usually hand embroidered by some worshiping dark-haired lady with a rose behind her ear.

1. This chiripa was made out of some bordered Indian cotton measuring 36" x 74" (that's just 2" over 2 yards). Soft fabric is best to use as it will drape nicely. The two ties measure 47" each. The ties pull the whole thing together.

2. Pleat in each end of chiripa fabric to 26", then sew the ribbon over it.

3. First tie a set of ribbons around to front of waist. Then, bringing fabric between legs, tie the remaining two ribbons apronlike to back of waist. Selvages finish garment at edges, so you need not hem it. Wear chiripa with legs bare or with tights.

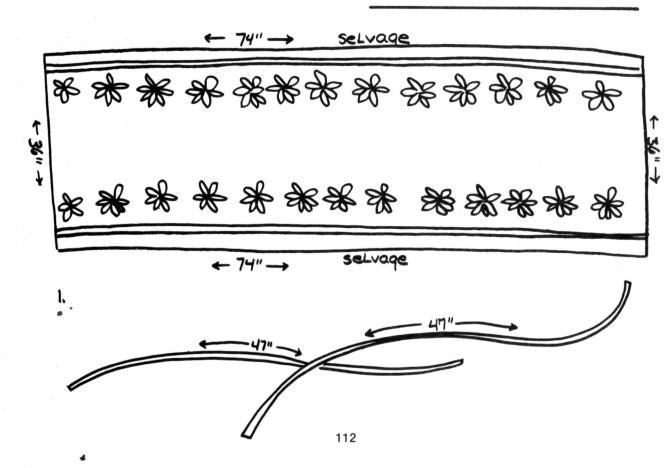

112

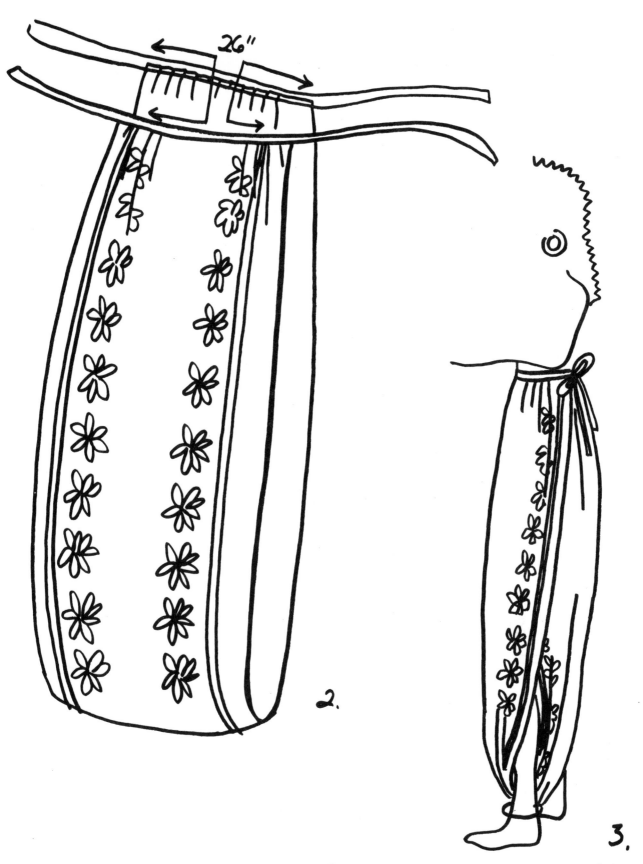

26"

2.

3.

The Fly-by-Night Dress

Like the chiripa, 36" fabric with selvages for finished edges works out nicely for this dress. Here, too, the ties "form" the dress.

1. Use one piece of fabric 36" x 106". Fold fabric in half widthwise. Cut a 15" slash widthwise directly in middle of fold for neckline. Hemstitch neckline. Hemstitch fabric at bottom edge. Slip garment over head. Locate spots where waistline falls on either side of garment. At those spots attach ribbons long enough to tie around body and sash in back.

2. Tie ribbons underneath back flap for cape effect.

3. Or, tie ribbons over back flap catching it underneath.

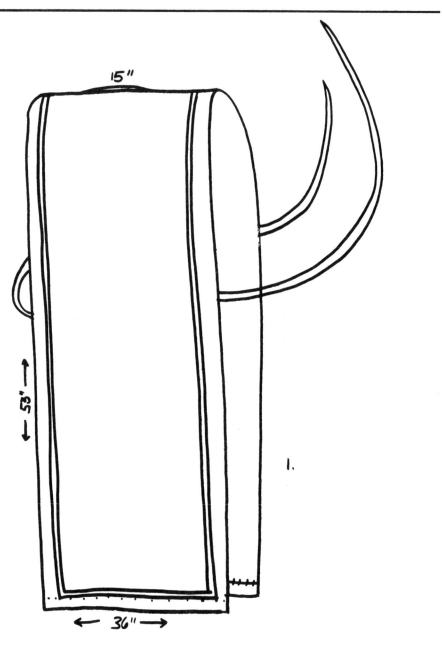

15"

53"

36"

1.

2.

3.

The Little Pregnant Number

Here two pieces of fabric are sewn together, and the entire garment is pulled into shape with the drawstrings.

1. Use fabric 36″ or 45″ wide, depending on fullness you want. If you are eight months pregnant you'll probably want 45″ wide fabric. Cut garment as long or as short as you'll want dress to be. Seam up side allowing 11″ on each side for armholes plus 1″ or 1 1/2″, whatever your preference, to turn under and seam at top to make casing for drawstrings. Insert drawstrings, long enough to amply tie on each shoulder, into casings. Hemstitch hem. Selvages will "finish" armholes unless you want to hemstitch them, too.

2. Tie garment over each shoulder after gathering dress together with drawstrings.

This garment is attractive on nonpregnant ladies, too.

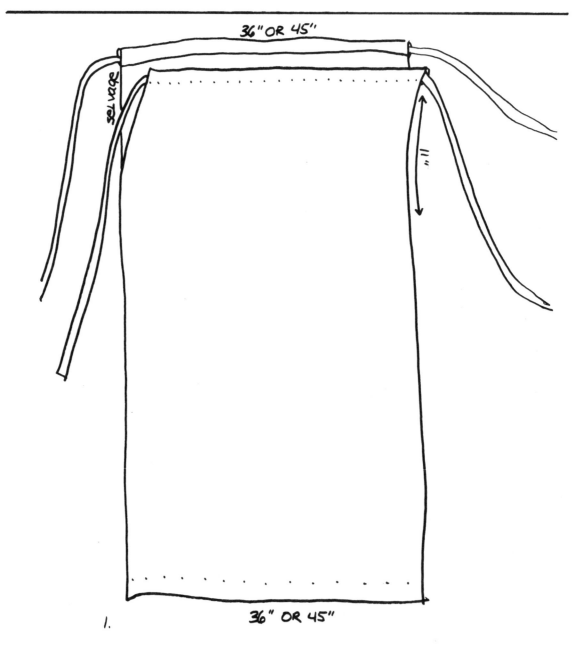

36″ OR 45″

selvage

11″

1.

36″ OR 45″

2.

Mexican Peasant Drawstring Dress One

This is a type of drawstring peasant dress similar to those worn in Mexico. With some experimentation, I've come up with the following way of making the garment. I've found it best to first make a paper pattern in the following manner.

1. Take two sheets of brown wrapping paper, or newspaper. Measure both sheets across broadest part of shoulder (see Figure 1). Cut width of paper allowing about 3" on either side of it. Cut paper's length to about 3'. Fold two sheets of paper as indicated in illustration. Snip edges of paper at points indicated with dotted lines. Then cut away paper at fold indicated by arrow. Now you have two sleeve pattern pieces the shape of Figure 1A. Fold sleeve pattern pieces in half along dotted line.

2. Sleeve pattern pieces will match body pattern piece (when both are cut into fabric) with AB seamed to EF; CD seamed to GH on both sides.

3. Garment can remain in the shape of a blouse, as shown in illustration, or can be made into a dress by first extending pattern out from blouse shape as dotted lines indicate. You can extend dress pattern 6" to 1' out on either side. Make it as long or as short as you wish. Place paper patterns onto fabric and cut out sleeve pieces allowing for a 1/2" seam all around on sleeves and body of blouse or dress.

Right sides of fabric together, seam both sleeve points A and B to body of garment points E and F. Again, right sides together seam points C and D to points G and H. Right sides of garment together, seam from outer edge under arm indicated by arrows down side seam to hem. Face neckline and make casings. Turn back and hem sleeves. Make a small slash at center front of dress through which drawstring will be pulled. Make two small slashes in sleeves, either at top of them or at front. Hemstitch slash. Edge neckline and sleeves with lace or eyelet, if you like. Draw a ribbon or cord through casings to pull dress into shape.

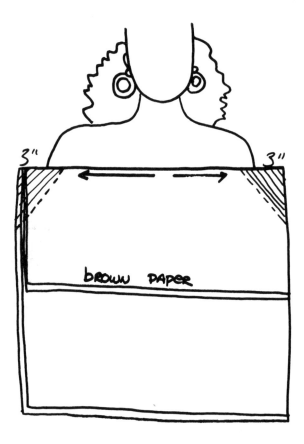

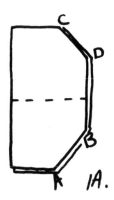

118

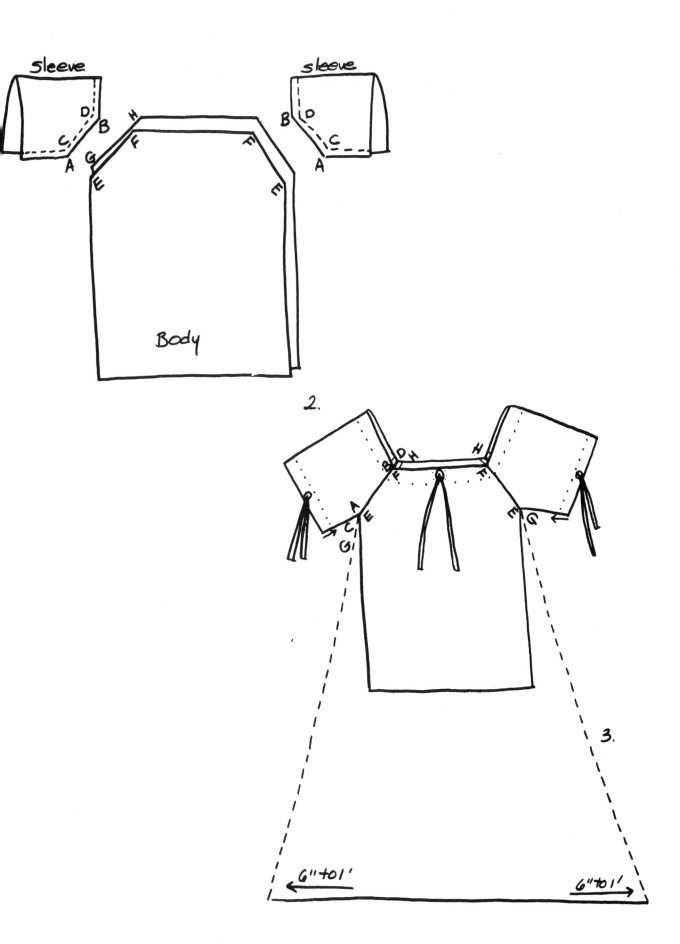

sleeve

sleeve

Body

2.

3.

6"to 1'   6"to 1'

4. Hemstitch dress.

4.

Mexican Peasant Drawstring Dress
Two

1. Fold 2 yards of 45" wide fabric lengthwise. Add a 1/2 yard to length if you want a long dress. Mark a point 7" in from selvage side and another point 4" down toward hem. Mark another point 4" down on fold edge. Connect points with a straightedge. This area will be cut away to make neckline. Mark a point 8" down on selvage side. 4" down from this point mark another one. Then 4" in from this point mark another one. Connect these 2 points with a diagonal line, which will measure about 5". Mark a point in 4" from bottom edge. With a straightedge ruler **draw a** straight line from end of 5" diagonal line to hemline. Cut away excess fabric at neckline and sides indicated with diagonal lines in illustration. A 62" ribbon or cord will later be used for drawstrings.

2. Right sides together, seam dress along both shoulder lines. Press. Seam bottoms of sleeves and down sides of dress. Clip a small wedge under each sleeve so that dress will not bunch up under arms when worn. Hemstitch hem. Leave selvages to finish sleeves or hemstitch them.

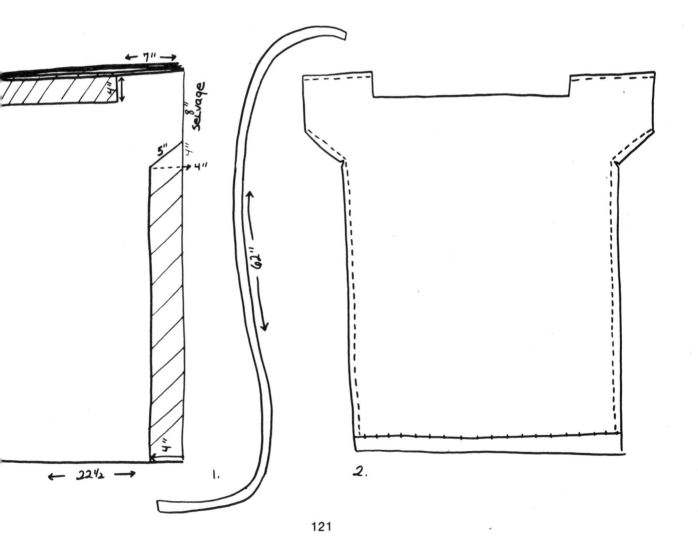

3. Topstitch a grosgrain ribbon casing around outside of dress neckline. Cut and seam ribbon to make corners as in Figure 3. Make a small insert in front of casing through which to run drawstring.

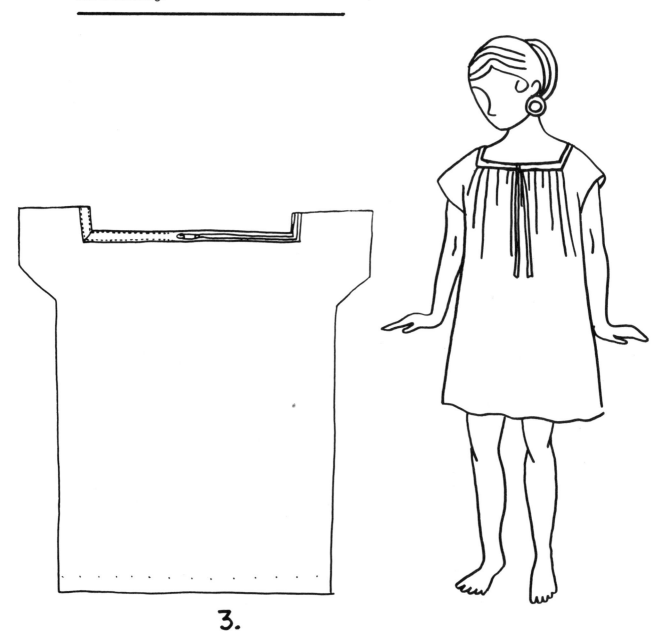

3.

Drawstring Top

1. First take bosom measurement. Then add 4" to that figure for ease and seams. If, for example, your measurement is 34", the total would be 38". Then measure from shoulder to point on hip where you want top to end, plus 1" for hem. Figure this is 25" for a top (there is a much longer allowance if you want to make a dress). Cut fabric 38" x 25". Seam along open side. Press. Now, you have a tubular piece of fabric. Measure from base of neck (at side) to armpit. Allow 2" extra for comfort. With seam in back, cut a V shape (about 13" long) down middle of each side. The top of V should be 7" across. Turn raw edges of V under and stitch them down.

2. Then turn top of both front and back down 1 1/2" to make a casing, and run two drawstrings through it (20" long), which will tie on each shoulder.

Drawstring Baggy Pants

I find these pants great to conceal a slightly protruding tummy, but my niece Andrea, who's skinny as a rail, looks great in them, too.

1. Cut four pieces exactly alike as shown in Figure 1. Cut the curve from A to B using a pair of old jeans as a pattern. The curve will measure approximately 14" and will fit most sizes as the pants are meant to be very loose. Pants will measure 12" across the top and across the bottom of pant leg. Cut pant length to suit your height, measuring from top, allowing room so pants almost cover shoes, but won't drag on ground. Then allow for a 2 1/2" hem. Use 46" drawstring to run through waistline casing.

2. Sew two pieces together along curves to make a front piece and other two pieces together to make back piece. Press. Now you have two parts to deal with not four. Right sides together, seam inseams of two pants parts as well as outside edges. Press. Hemstitch bottom of pants. Turn under waistline edge and hemstitch. Make a 3/4" opening inside front pants seam to insert drawstring.

3. Run drawstring through waistline seam and draw together britches. Fasten a safety pin at one end to lead the drawstring through the open seam.

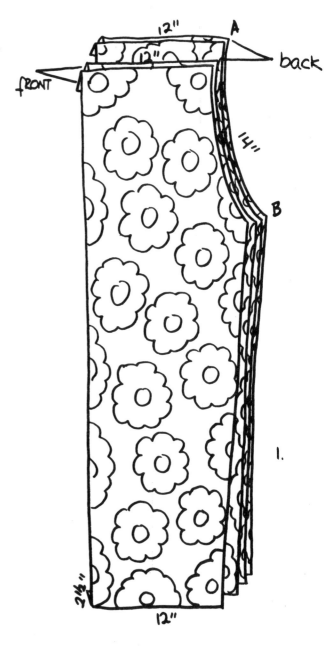

1.

124

inside

2.

3.

4. To dress up drawstring pants, add a deep flounce to them. To make flounce, measure from 2" above knee to edge of pants, allowing 2 1/2 for a hem. Use about twice as much fabric for each ruffle as used for each pant leg. After hemming fabric, sew into tubes. Then press down a 1/4" edge at top of each tube. Gather top of each tube to make it flouncy around bottom. Then pull flounce up over each pant leg and topstitch in place. If you topstitch by hand, it may be easier to remove stitches to convert pants back and forth from the plain drawstring to the flounced version.

All Around Wraparound Skirt

This skirt would be fabulous for the first few months of pregnancy as you could keep loosening the tie a little each time you expanded a bit. But, don't think of this simply as a maternity and postpartum skirt. I think it's great looking in its own right for any woman from the skinniest little lady to the roundest one.

1. First make a brown paper pattern. And, to be extra sure about fit, make up a rough sample in muslin. To get a correct measurement for pattern do the following: First take waist measurement. Let's say it's 24". Divide that by 3, giving yourself a figure of 8. As in Figure 1, mark brown paper beginning at bottom with two spaces measuring 8". Then, alternate 24", then 8", ending up with two spaces of 8" at end. From left-hand corner at top of paper, measure over 24". Alternate to 8", etc. These figures will change in proportion to your waist measurement. Then with a ruler connect figures on top and bottom of brown paper as indicated in illustration. Measure length of brown paper used for diagram to find amount of fabric needed for skirt. Add 5" for seam allowances. Cut paper pattern pieces along diagonal lines.

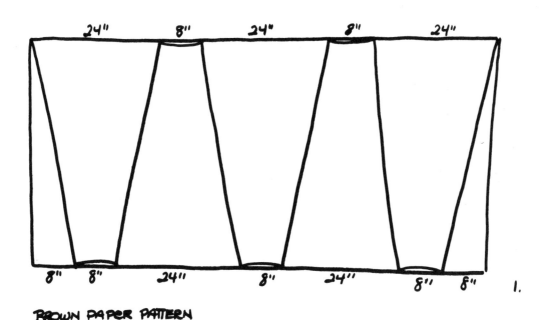

BROWN PAPER PATTERN

1.

2. Lay pattern pieces out on fabric as in illustration. Allow for 1/2'' seams around each piece. Cut out pieces as indicated by broken lines.

3. Right sides together, seam all pieces, leaving a 1'' space for a ribbon hole at point A in Figure 3. Hemstitch this space. Press open all seams. Hemstitch bottom of skirt 2 1/2'' and sides 1''. Attach a grosgrain ribbon (measuring twice waist circumference) around waistline of skirt. Ribbon will draw from back of skirt through space A at side seam. It then ties together with ribbon from other side of skirt.

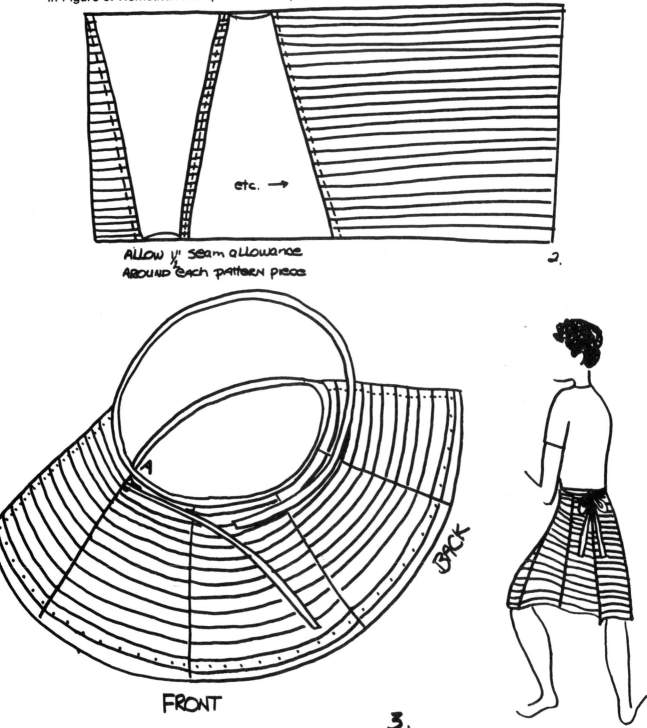

etc. →

ALLOW 1'' seam allowance
AROUND each pattern piece

2.

A

FRONT

BACK

3.

Wraparound Pantskirt

1. You'll need about 3 yards for this pantskirt, maybe only 2 1/2 if you use 45" wide fabric. Fold fabric in half widthwise. Cut a front and a back piece from a well-fitting old pair of jeans. Pin pieces down at center of doubled fabric to get correct "crotchline." Mark crotchline lightly with a pencil and cut away excess fabric. (If shaky about cutting directly into cloth, make a paper or muslin pattern first.)

2. Stitch along crotchline. Then, clip seams so pantskirt won't bunch up in this area when you wear it.

3. Figure 3 shows how jeans are used to measure shape of pantskirt. (We all know, of course, they are not actually incorporated into design.) For the top, you measure pantskirt out 6" from front and back jeans pattern pieces. And for the bottom, again you measure 6" out from jeans pattern pieces, plus add 6" for flare. Fabric is marked diagonally on each edge with a yardstick. Excess material is cut away. Allow 2 1/2" for hem and

hemstitch. Attach ties A and B & C and D (grosgrain ribbon or self fabric) to front and then to back of pantskirt. Ties must be long enough to wrap "apron-style" around to back.

4. Bring ties C and D around to front.

5. Tie ties C and D together at front to hold garment together.

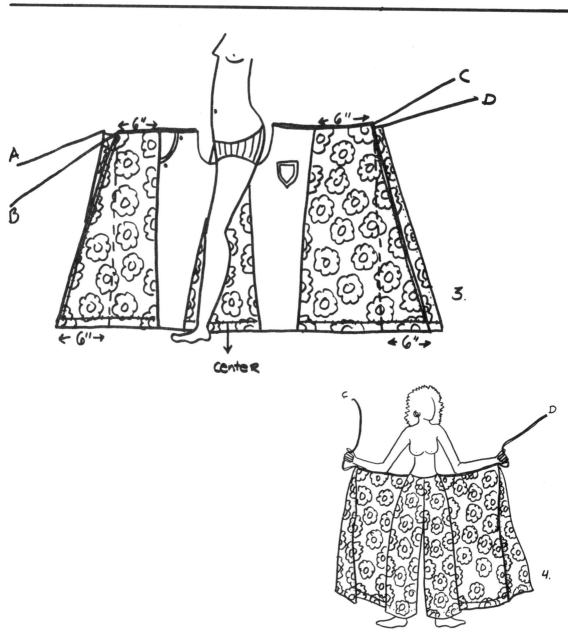

5.

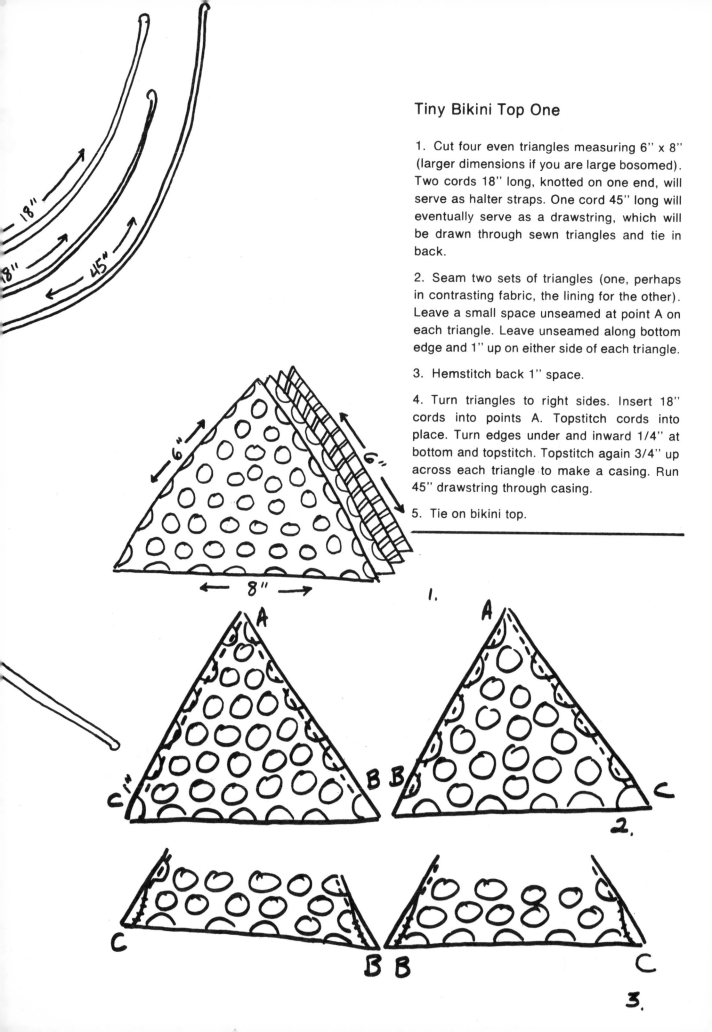

Tiny Bikini Top One

1. Cut four even triangles measuring 6'' x 8'' (larger dimensions if you are large bosomed). Two cords 18'' long, knotted on one end, will serve as halter straps. One cord 45'' long will eventually serve as a drawstring, which will be drawn through sewn triangles and tie in back.

2. Seam two sets of triangles (one, perhaps in contrasting fabric, the lining for the other). Leave a small space unseamed at point A on each triangle. Leave unseamed along bottom edge and 1'' up on either side of each triangle.

3. Hemstitch back 1'' space.

4. Turn triangles to right sides. Insert 18'' cords into points A. Topstitch cords into place. Turn edges under and inward 1/4'' at bottom and topstitch. Topstitch again 3/4'' up across each triangle to make a casing. Run 45'' drawstring through casing.

5. Tie on bikini top.

A   A

C   B B   C

4.

5

Tiny Bikini Top Two

1. Cut two right triangles, each measuring 25" on the straight edge, 27" on the diagonal side, 1" on the top and 9" to 10" on the bottom. (Triangles can be made wider and longer to fit a very ample bosom.) Cut 25" sides on the selvages, if possible. Stitch under 1/4" along tops and diagonal sides. Gather bottom until it comfortably fits around bosom. Hold it against you to adjust gathering. For tie, cut a strip of fabric 4' long and 3" wide. Turn under each end 1/4" and topstitch. Press 4' length in half, then press under 1/2" on each side.

2. Find center of tie. Put the gathers of each triangle (straight edges of triangles facing toward center front) into folds of tie. Pin up 1/2" seam allowances on either side of gathers of both triangles. Topstitch from one end of tie to the other, securing the gathers as you go. Tie tiny bikini top around neck and at back.

Both this and the Tiny Bikini Top One go with bikini bottom that follows.

Little Bikini Bottom

First make bikini bottom up in muslin, for trial fit. Then adjustments can be made.

1. To get your correct size for bikini bottom begin by taking hip measurement. Say it is 34". Add 1" to that figure for seams for a total of 35". Divide that figure in half. Then add 1" to back and subtract 1" from front. Now back equals 18 1/2", front equals 16 1/2". (If you want to have more of a gap for skin to show through at sides where bikini will tie, snip off an inch before casting on ties and sewing pieces together.) To get bathing suit depth, measure from center of crotch to how high you want bathing suit to come. Same goes for back. Then allow another 1" for seams at top and bottom: say, front equals 10", make it 11"; back equals 13", make it 14". Measurement across width of crotch is 3". Now draw curved lines connecting side seams to crotch, curving back line slightly to allow for fullness

of fanny. Cut out lining just like outside. (Both outside and lining material should be lightweight cotton, or a blend.)

2. Put right sides together, sew front and back piece of bikini bottom across 3" crotchline. Do the same with front and back lining pieces. Press open seams. To attach ties (two on each side of front, two on each side of back) pin them facing inward. Now sew front part of bikini to lining. Lay them out right sides together (see Figure 2). Ties will now be between front part and lining. Pin together and stitch all around (catching ties in seams). Leave space A to B unseamed so bikini bottom can be turned to right side at this point. Ties will now be on outside so you can fasten bikini together. Press bikini, ironing under a 1/2" seam on side that was left open for turn. Pin ties securely in this section and topstitch.

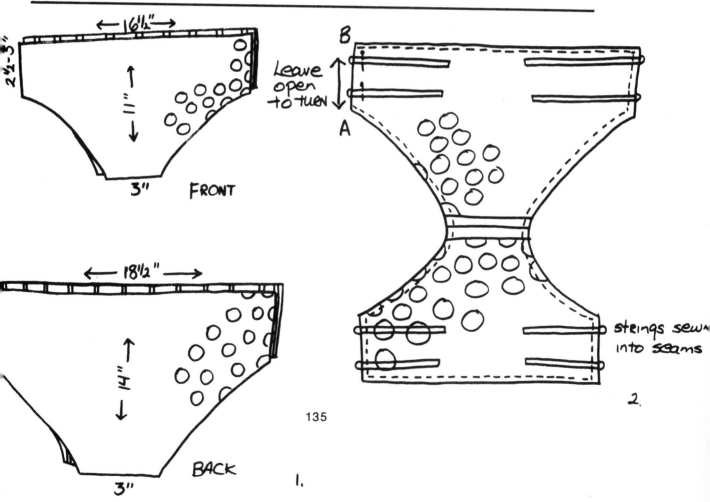

135

3. To even out topstitching effect you can repeat on all sides. Tie on bikini bottom. If sides have been trimmed back you'll have more skin showing through, as in illustration.

3

10. ...And More

Like my friend Billy Brauer said, when much to his surprise he learned that he a city-bred kid from Queens could be a master carpenter in Vermont, "We've been taught that 'other people' make things and that we buy them." Fortunately a lot of us are re-thinking the consumer theory.

The clothes patterns given in the preceding chapters will keep you from "going naked," sure enough. But, more than that, hopefully these patterns, and the friends who sent many of them, have taught you that *you can sew.* You can sew quickly, easily, and in-expensively. You don't, in fact, even need to use the patterns in this book. You can invent your own patterns by wrapping on a piece of cloth, seaming it into a tube, piecing together a few geometric shapes, and/or pulling the whole thing together with ties or drawstrings.

You can make gifts by sewing, even make money. You can make your own hat, bags, and more . . . coming up.

$$3.14\overline{)22}\,\,^{7\,(Rounded\ off)}$$

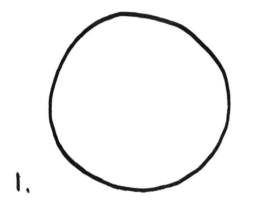

1.

Handcrafted Floppy Hat

This hat can be made up in felt or soft leather, which you may or may not sew up by hand (using heavy-gauge thread), depending upon whether your sewing machine is sturdy enough. On the other hand, my machine is an old Singer featherweight and it will sew through a lightweight leather.

1. Cut a circle the circumference of your head (here 22'' is used as standard).

2. Cut a strip measuring circumference of head on inside and 4'' wide. Topstitch strip together.

3. Topstitch circle inside seamed strip to make crown.

4. Cut brim 6'' wide and 1'' less than circumference of head, as you will be clipping back 1'' wedges to fit brim into crown.

5. Fit the 1'' wedges into crown and topstitch.

6. For decoration, attach ribbon or flower to hat.

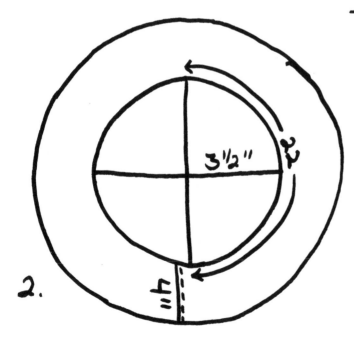

2.

3½''

1" for seam allowance

3.

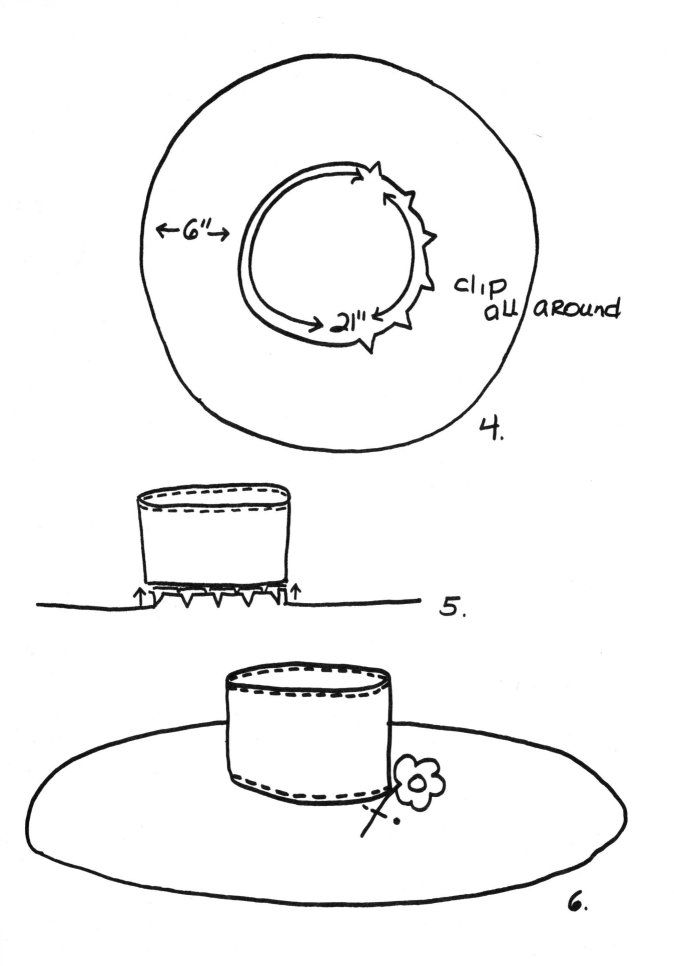

←6"→

21"

clip all around

4.

5.

6.

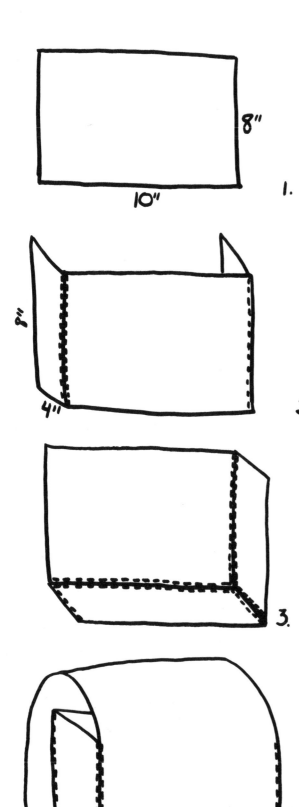

Handcrafted Boxy Bag

This bag can be sewn by machine or hand, using a heavy-gauge thread. Heavy-gauge machine needles can be bought at Singer sewing machine stores.

1. Cut a piece of felt, vinyl, or leather 8" x 10" for central bag piece.

2. Cut two side pieces 8" x 4". Topstitch to central bag piece.

3. Cut bottom piece 4" x 10". Topstitch to central and side pieces.

4. Cut a back-to-flap piece 10" x 8". Topstitch at back along bottom and up side edges. Leave rest of flap open.

5. Cut a strap piece 3" by whatever length you want it to be: longer to wear over shoulder, shorter for over arm. Topstitch to sides of bag.

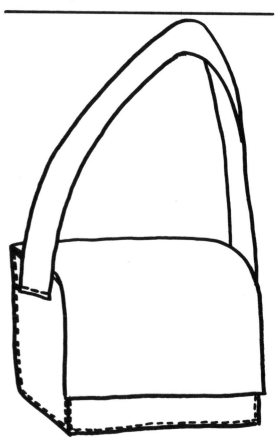

Woven Ribbon Tote

1. Cut several grosgrain ribbons of one color, yellow for example, according to the width you prefer for tote. Pin ribbons down (as many as you desire depth of tote to be), on either end, to a solid surface. Then choose contrasting grosgrain ribbon, blue for example. Cut several strips of blue to match the depth of ribbons pinned down horizontally, plus a 2" to 2 1/2" overlap on each end. Begin weaving the blue ribbons over and under the pinned-down yellow ribbons, moving one row, after it has been woven, tightly up against the next, until the entire area has been woven.

Then, unpin ribbons from surface and top-stitch to hold in place. Repeat this process to make a second side exactly the same as the first. Stitch two sides of grosgrain ribbons together to make two handles for tote.

2. Seam the two woven ribbon pieces together at bottom and sides, stitching as close to edge of ribbons, near topstitching, as possible. Clip back excess ribbon to 1/2 to 1". Clip back top ribbons to 1 1/2". Stitch under 1/4". Hemstitch top ribbons to inside of tote. Attach ribbon handles to ends of each side of tote.

1.

2.

Mrs. Geist's Puff-Piece Vest and Bag

Ella Geist, who lives on a farm in North Dakota, makes puff pieces from quilt scraps, this way no fabric goes to waste. (Note: use cutaway parts of circular designs, pantskirt, and so forth.)

1. Cut scraps into many small circles the same size—2 1/2" in diameter is fine. Sew a running stitch around outside edge of each circle.

2. Tighten up running stitch gathers as in Figure 2. Gathers will "pull in" diameter size of circles. Press puff pieces flat. The sides with gathers will face outward from body when vest is completed, and to outside when it is finished.

3. Sew gathered puff pieces together, attaching them with small tacking stitches.

4. Cut a paper pattern to the size and shape of garment, or anything else you want to make. Here a vest and a tote are shown. Cut a lining to fit the vest or tote and stitch puff pieces to it. You can stitch each puff piece individually to the lining. Or, you can stitch the edge of the entire group of puff pieces to the edge of lining. Or, leave puff pieces alone, without lining, so you can see through the spaces between them. A vest, of course, is better unlined than a tote, which needs the extra strength of the lining.

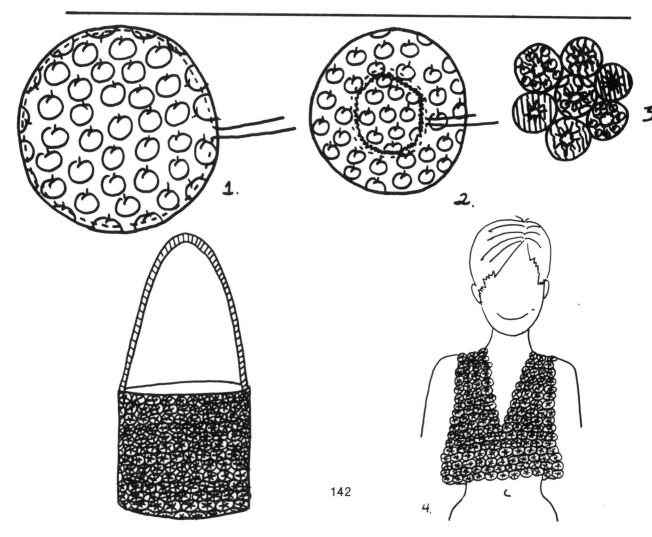

1.

2.

3

4.

142

Mrs. Geist's Harvest Bib

1. Cut a rectangular shape that measures from waist to collarbone and is wide as an apron bib. Then cut out a curved shape at top of rectangle. Hem back curved shape at top. Sew grosgrain ribbons to sides of bib to finish edges and to tie it around neck. Sew another ribbon at bottom of bib to tie it around waist.

The most fun is decorating bib, which you do before attaching ribbons. It can be embroidered or appliqued. Laces and rickracks can be sewn to it. This bib is particularly pretty for little girls to wear over sweaters with pants or skirts. But, grown-up ladies look nice in it, too.

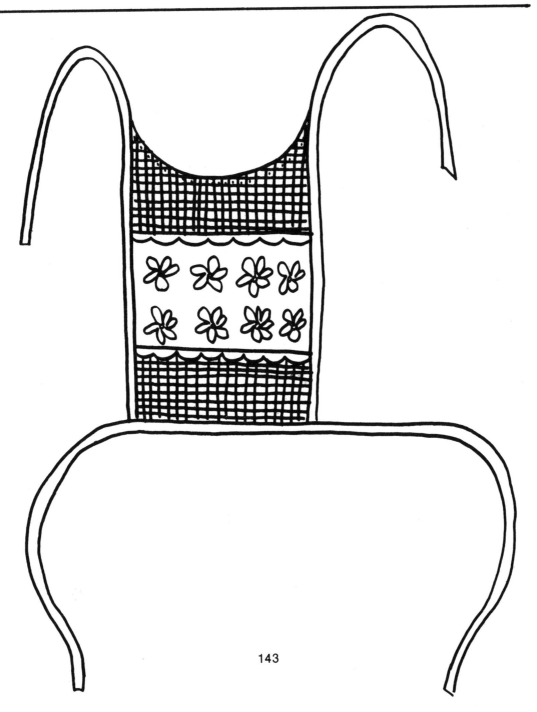

Pretty Carpet Slippers

1. First make a muslin pattern of slippers to get accurate fit. They are tricky. Then, make them up in suede or felt. And embroider them, if you like. First trace the sole of your foot on paper. Mark letters on it at points indicated in Figure 1. Transfer to muslin and again mark letters.

2. Hold a piece of muslin over top of foot marking points around toes where it would reach slipper sole. Then mark points where muslin reaches around sides of foot, all the way to points marked A on sole pattern. These points will be marked A on slipper top pattern, too. Mark X at point where slipper top covers foot sufficiently. Using guidelines made by your own foot, cut a shape that corresponds roughly to that of Figure 2. Area AXA can be curved out if you later want a rounder shape.

3. Hold a piece of muslin around heel, mark a point O where it corresponds with O on muslin sole. Bring muslin around to sides of foot and mark BB where it matches up with AA. Cut a shape that corresponds roughly to that of Figure 3.

4. Quickly sew muslin pieces together as in Figure 4. Adjust pattern sizes until they correctly fit foot. Then transfer pattern to suede or felt.

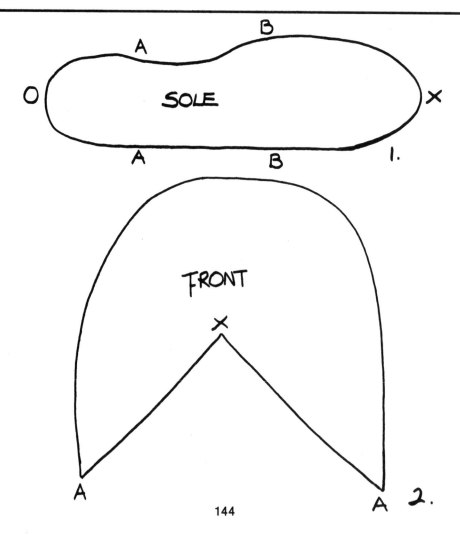

144

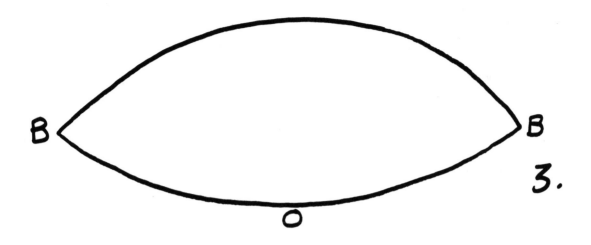

B   B

3.

O

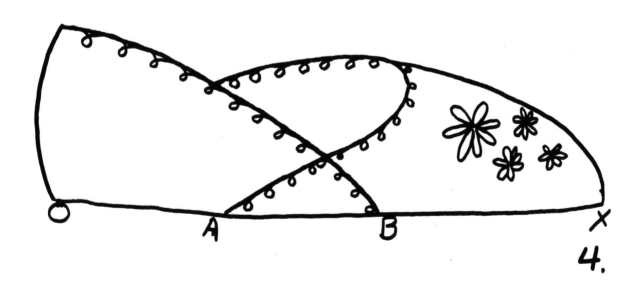

O   A   B   X

4.

145

Guatemalan Handbag

1. Cut two rectangular pieces of fabric 7" x 13". Hemstitch at top. Cut a strip of fabric 7" x 60" and press it in half lengthwise. Cut two strips of cloth 7" x 6" and fringe 2" at bottom. Lengthwise seam each strip together and turn to right side to press.

2. Sew 60" strip to two rectangular pieces. Right sides together, begin at point A on one rectangle and point A on strip. Then, right sides together, begin at point C on strip and point C on rectangle, seam two pieces together. Repeat these steps matching up and seaming points B and D on second rectangle and other side of strip. Hem back either side of folded strip. Press up 1" all around bottom of bag.

3. Turn bag to right side. Insert fringed strips into each side of bag. Pin to secure. Topstitch from one end of bag to the other, enclosing fringed strips. Embroider or decorate bag in any manner you like.

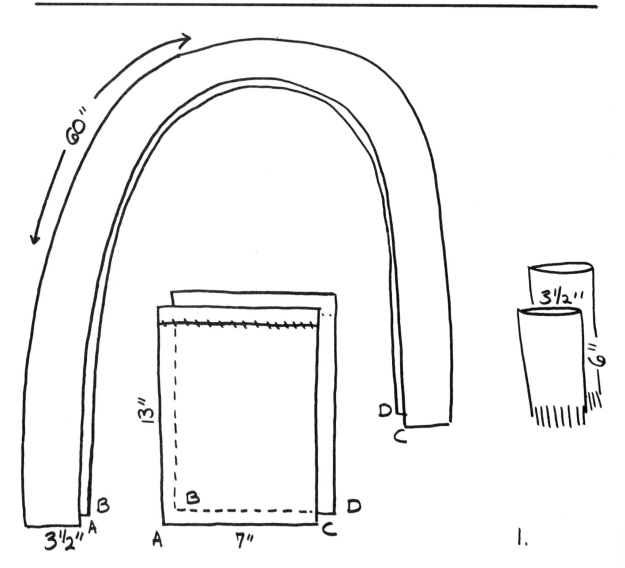

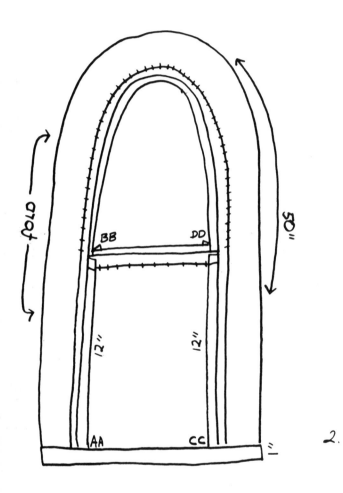

BB   DD

fold

50"

12"   12"

AA   CC

1"

2.

50" TOTAL ALL WAY AROUND

FOLD ALL WAY AROUND

12"

3"   6"   3"

5½"   5½"

3.

Dear Tim:

I've been thinking about you a lot lately, what with doing nothing but that sewing book day in and day out for months now. I can't honestly say I've found the time to lie down on my Indian print bedspread and cut a dress out around me. For that matter, every time I lie down on the damn thing I fall asleep. The book's been fun, but . . .

Actually I'm pretty addicted to making all those snappy dresses and things my friends have told me about. I've tried each and every one of them, and now I'm the best-dressed writer sitting down to any typewriter in town. However, there are still some days when I'm here all alone and don't even bother to dress. That's pure literary freedom, wouldn't you say? But then, most times, I pull out my "pattern for the day," whip up a quicky number in muslin, make us all some bread, then sit down to write. Of course, those are the times when the whole family's around, when you can't go naked.

We'd all love to see you soon. . . . Maybe at the Phoenix again the next time it snows in Sugarbush.

Love,

Summer of '73

Donna

148